Dynamic Memory

Success in Exams with Better Marks

(Be a Perfect Student)

Vijay Anand

DIAMOND BOOKS

Published by : **Diamond Pocket Books (P) Ltd.**
X-30, Okhla Industrial Area, Phase-II
New Delhi-110020
Phone : 011-40712200

E-mail : wecare@diamondbooks.in
Website : www.diamondbooks.in
Edition : 2024
Printed by : Repro (India)

DYNAMIC MEMORY SUCCESS IN EXAMS WITH BETTER MARKS
(BE A PERFECT STUDENT) By - Vijay Anand

INTRODUCTION

Historically, the term 'student' is referred to anyone who learns something. However, according to the common definition, a 'student' is anyone who attends school, college, or university.

Today's students are tomorrow's leaders and the qualities of the student clearly determine the students' future and carrier path. So, who is a good student? What are the qualities of a good student?

A good student is not always the student who gets an A grade. Some students can get an 'A' grade with a little effort and usually take any path they need to, to get that 'A'. Then there are those students who work their little hearts out and get 'B' grade or even sometimes 'C' grade even if they are much better students than those who get 'A' grade. Thus, a student is someone who wants to learn and study to make himself better.

Self Discipline is of the utmost importance. If a student lacks this quality, then few other qualities will be found in him. Self-discipline means that before speaking and acting, one thinks and then makes choices that are right for him and for others. Those with self-discipline accept that things do not always go their way.

Respect for others' and for property will be present in good students. They will treat others the way they want to be treated. Destroying or taking someone's property and harming, it would not be something they would do.

Perseverance can be found in good students. They will work hard and not give up when it gets tough. They stick to something until it is finished. In other words, they don't give up, but always keep trying.

Citizenship is found in good students. They obey the rules and work to make the community & school a better place.

Compassion is present in good students. They are kind toward others and help them instead of knocking them down verbally and physically.

Integrity is found in good students. They make choices that help them to be the best. They do what they think is right and work towards doing their best.

Responsibility is always present in good students. They are dependable and make good choices. They take care of things that belong to them and show more responsibility when they take care of themselves and what they do.

Trustworthiness is a must. These students can be counted on to do the right thing even if an adult is not present. They return borrowed items and do what they say they'll do.

Fairness is another trait present in good students. They will take turns, share and listen to what others say. They take only their share and play by the rules.

Honesty is found in good students. They are truthful and sincere. They will do their own work and return borrowed items. They are the ones who will make sure that their score is correct even if it means that they get more negatives.

If you find these qualities in you then without doubt, you are a perfect student in every aspect.

Contents

1

QUALITIES OF A GOOD STUDENT

Today's students are tomorrow's leaders and the qualities of the student clearly determine their future and carrier path. So, who is a good student? What are the qualities of a good student? Historically, the term 'student' is referred to anyone who learns something. However, the recent definition of a "student" is anyone who attends school, college, or university.

What makes a student stand out from the rest? The four **As**: **attitude, academic skills, awareness**, and **accomplishment**, certainly play a vital part in it, and a student who has all these traits will be very likely to earn As:

- Attitude is primarily a genuine desire to learn, and the willingness to do hard intellectual work to achieve understanding. It is also shown by the way you apply yourself even to those subjects in which you have little interest, and how much you achieve even when a professor's style isn't to your liking.
- Academic skills include ability to read with comprehension, intelligent use of resources (including library), logical and mathematical skills, efficient study habits, and the ability to communicate clearly and fluently -speaking and writing.
- Awareness of what's going on in the world around you, and the habit of intelligently relating it to your academic courses. For example, when taking a course in political science, you should relate what you are learning in class to what's happening on the national and world political scenario. When taking a science course, you should relate scientific principles to phenomena you observe in everyday life, and go out of your way to find applications and examples of science in the real world.

- Accomplishment is demonstrated by successful application of understanding. The evidence of that is:
  - o Correct and confident application of what you've learned to new problems and challenges.
  - o Clear and effective communication of your understanding through speaking and writing.
  - o Possession of a wealth of information, skills and understanding sufficient to allow you to continue your education outside the classroom, throughout your life.

OTHER QUALITIES OF A PERFECT STUDENT

Ability: A good student has the ability to apply the results of his or her learning in a creative way and achieve the goals.

Self-Discipline: Discipline in managing the time is an important factor that every good student must possess. Often, delaying the tasks, such as writing assignments, reading text books, etc. may negatively impact the ability of a student to achieve the goals.

Understanding rather than memorizing concepts: A lot of surveys suggest that students must understand the concepts rather than just memorizing them. The memorized facts and theories will stay in students' memory until they leave school, college, or university. Once out of school, the students will totally forget the core concepts that they have learned. Therefore, it is essential to a good student to understand the concepts.

Beside above mentioned qualities, a perfect student should have the following qualities:

- **Initiative.** In short, doing things without being told. The student doesn't wait for assignments to read ahead in the textbook, or to seek out and study related books to gain understanding. The good student does more problems or exercises than assigned, and does them even when none are assigned. The good student working in the laboratory does not merely follow instructions (though that is an important skill) but looks for opportunities to discover new things, try new things, or find better methods. When an opportunity arises to do a project outside the class, the good student jumps at the chance and doesn't even ask whether it will earn extra credit.
- **Breadth of interests.** College provides a great opportunity to broaden your interests and explore new things. You may never again have such a convenient and comprehensive library, such diverse and inexpensive cultural events and academic activities. Much of education can occur outside the class, if you seek it. But if you confine yourself to the things you've always done, avoiding anything new and unfamiliar, you will have squandered a valuable opportunity.
- An open mind is a mind receptive to examination of new ideas and facts. Having an open mind does *not* mean that one jumps on the bandwagon of every new fad. A better characterization of an open mind is one which is willing to analyze new ideas dispassionately and rationally, weighing them objectively against established knowledge and the facts at hand.
- **A critical habit of mind.** Education is more than the acquisition of information. It includes the ability to acquire new information, to critically evaluate that information, and to correctly and effectively use it. With so many sources of information at our disposal in this computer age, we are awash with information, and in danger of information overload. But much of the information is fraudulent, worthless, incomplete, or just plain wrong. It has always

been so. Probably 95% of the books in any library could be destroyed without harming human knowledge. But it's not easy to determine which books are worth keeping. We are virtually assaulted by folks trying to sell us something (with impressive claims of its value), to persuade us to accept some political or social idea, to convert us to another religion or philosophy, or to convince us of the value of some medical panacea. One of the values of a good education is the ability to see through false and unfounded claims and outright deceptions. By this criterion, education has largely been a failure, for many people who have college degrees are still suckers for the snake-oil and perpetual-motion-machine peddlers.

- **Perceptiveness.** The more you learn, the more perceptive you become. You can, as necessary, 'read between the lines.' You no longer need everything spelled out; you can fill in missing details. You aren't dependent on being shown; you can puzzle things out for yourself. You perceive quickly what a writer or speaker means, without misinterpreting. You learn to seek the intended meaning of what you read or hear rather than trying to impose your own preconceived meaning. You can see through complexity to the heart of a matter. You are able to distinguish the important from the trivial in a serious discussion.
- **Objectivity.** Most of us begin our education with an 'egocentric' view, expecting everything to have some relevance to our needs or desires. We even impose such interpretations on things we learn, and avoid learning some things because they don't seem important at the time. Education can broaden that view, encouraging us to set our egos aside and objectively evaluate facts and interpretations. We find out that mere unsupported personal opinions have no value in an academic discussion. We learn to recognize the validity of facts and ideas that we may not like. We learn that other people and other cultures interpret things differently, and that fact is not a-priori evidence that they are wrong. We learn that the world does not revolve around us, and the universe cares not a bit whether we exist, or what we do. Education can give us humility.

- **Humility.** However much one learns, one must realize there's a lot more to be learned, and that some of what one 'knows' may turn out to be wrong. For this reason intellectual arrogance is unbecoming an educated person. Knowing lots of things is good, but knowing the limitations of one's knowledge is essential to using it properly. Many of the classic errors of history were made by people over-confidently going beyond what they knew and understood.

Inborn abilities, talents mean a lot when you want to study and get knowledge or profession. But inborn talents can not guarantee that one will become a really good or let alone perfect student. Nothing can be achieved without taking efforts, without thoughtful and thorough approach to what you are doing. You need to be self-disciplined and must know how to balance between studying and rest in order to make your studying process most efficient and fruit-bearing. Anyone who wants to become a good student should know that he may face a lot of difficulties. Not always we learn something new easily, because it requires time, patience and diligence. However, if you are sure about your purpose, you should concentrate and work hard for achieving best results.

❑❑❑

2

MANAGE TIME

You are a student and trying your best to cope up with time pressure, there is one important thing you should always remember—work smarter and not harder.

Managing time is a skill which can be mastered by thinking and acting smartly. Many times students put in great efforts in improving their time management skills, but at the end they realize that no matter how much effort they put. They always end up defeated in attaining the goals they set. This is the result of working hard on managing their time.

What do you mean by being smart in time management? You do not have to increase your efforts. You only have to focus twice as hard the first time so you do not need a second or third attempt. If you can avoid multiple attempts, you save a lot of time and your schedule remains on track too.

You just have to be ahead of your plans and double the efforts needed. This is how smart time management works. If students learn how to make this work, they will be able to keep up and survive the demanding academic life that they are facing.

COMMON MISTAKES IN TIME MANAGMENT

Often, students encounter some mistakes in their overall time management skills that can hinder or even stop them from making their way smoothly towards the attainment of goals.

Starting the day without an action plan: The most important thing in time management is doing things right and not doing it fast. The latter just results in spoiling your valuable time. It is best to have a specific goal for the day. What do you want to accomplish? How will you go about accomplishing those things?

Begin doing when the day begins. So you can attain your tasks by the end of the day.

No stability in life: It is said that life is comprised of seven important areas. These are family, health, intellectual, financial, professional, social and spiritual. As a student, you cannot spend equal amount of time to all these things. There may be some areas where you need to focus more on a certain day and other areas for a different day.

All these areas are related to each other. One cannot work properly without being dependent on some. That is why you need to balance your time in different areas to be more stable and at peace.

It may seem difficult initially to adjust your time in all the areas of your life. But you can attend to all areas if you plan your time properly.

Untidy and chaotic study area: Ever noticed that when there are a lot of things around you, you get distracted easily? Not only you lose your concentration and your mind starts drifting away from work, you lose the enthusiasm and feel sad while studying.

Compare this to a clean and arranged area. You will not feel buried among the mess and can focus on the task at hand.

This is the same reason that office workers are effective. You do not see any mess lying around their work place much. They maintain a clean and cluster free environment. So it will be easy to move around without any distractions. This same principle should be applied to your study area.

Not enough sleep: According to studies, almost 75% of students constantly complain of being tired easily. Some even get tired even before the day is finished. It is not that they lack any sleep. A few are even disciplined enough to get the 8-10 hours sleep that is needed. What is lacking in them is quantity and quality sleep.

It seems that students are so stressed throughout the day; that they find it difficult to get a full night's sleep after studying hard.

Try to put away all your worries and problems when you go to bed. Remember, when you tackle one thing at a time, you will be at your best. Think only about sleep when you sleep. You will notice that you can sleep easily. In the morning, you will feel refreshed and ready to tackle the day with a clear and focused mind.

Lot of times stress causes you not to sleep and follow your time calendar. If you were not stressful, you could have worked as per schedule. Sometimes speculations of problems also cause stress. In such scenario, think and list down all your worries and concerns that cause stress. You will find things are not as stressful as you thought they are.

As a student, you have an advantage of early learning when you try to master time management skills. You can commit mistakes too, it's just that you should learn from them and find your way out.

❑❑❑

3

TIME MANAGEMENT FOR SCHOOL STUDENTS

Everyone understands how heavily occupied school students stay throughout their high school days. They need to focus on so many important school activities at the same time and still need to keep time for family and friends.

If you are a high school student, you know how difficult it is to complete your daily work. You even wished there were more hours in a day! Days pass by so fast that before you realize it, the day gets over and your studies remain unfinished.

However, everything you need to accomplish in a day is possible if you are organized and plan everything accordingly. Managing your time is not as difficult as it seems.

Here are some time management tips for you to follow to make high school life easier and have extra time for you, your friends and family:

Set goals everyday – Before you sleep, list down all the things you want to accomplish on the next day. This will help you know what you are going to do and avoid doing unimportant tasks. With a 'to do' list, you will get everything done more efficiently and faster.

Prioritize your list of goals – You know what is the most important task to complete from the 'to do' list you made. Try to prioritize the activities you want to achieve.

Similar to daily 'to-do' list, you can also make a list of goals you want to achieve in life. Put your most important goal in life on the top of your priority list and your least important goals to down below the list. Now, adjust your planner so that your activities match with your goals. It is also important that you should be realistic on your list, try to base your list on what you need to achieve and not on what you want to achieve. If you have a long-term priority, it is probably best that you put it on the bottom of your list; you can always work on that tomorrow.

Use your spare time – You may not notice it but you have lots of spare time as a high school student. Try to add up the minutes of the bus ride to school and the ride back home.

You can use these times to study and do your homework. By doing this, you will get an idea on what you need to do on your homework when you get home. This allows you to finish your homework faster and have extra time for other things.

Finding the right time – Students have the 'right time' to study. Students have specific time to study more efficiently. For example, you solved your math problems on afternoons; do not wait until night to do it. When your mood shifts immediately start solving math problems as much as you can before losing interest.

Taking notes – Writing down important notes is an effective way to study. It is much better than just plain reading. Writing down notes has an effect on your mind. You can understand and memorize the topic more effectively than by just reading. It is also important that you review your notes as your teacher might give a quiz on the next day. Reviewing your notes will help you to be more prepared for the quizzes that your teacher may suddenly give.

Get enough sleep – Studying during sleep will affect our health.

If you need to sleep you have to sleep, do not force yourself to study. If you try to study in this situation, you will most likely to waste your time.

Above tips should assist you in improving your time management skills. It will make your journey through school life more enjoyable. Keep faith in yourself and your abilities to meet your goals. If you plan properly and set aside enough time for rest, there is no one who can stop you from achieving your goals. Just make sure that you have planned your time realistically.

❑ ❑ ❑

4

UNDERSTAND VALUE OF TIME

Do you fall behind in your homework and other school activities? Are you one of the last students to finish your school projects? If 24 hours in a day seem insufficient to you to complete your work, don't think that you are a dull student, you just need some preparation and training in time management. You can achieve your daily goals efficiently by practicing time management skills.

Mismanagement of time is a common problem found in school students. When students do not find enough time for studies or they stress out due to lack of good results, it shows how poorly they manage their time.

Below are some suggestions on how best you can manage your time and start organizing your messy and hectic life.

Make it a point to list things you need to do: Priority is the keyword. List down the tasks you want to complete in a day from top to low priority. You can also use a planner or calendar for this. After finishing one task, go for the next. Before you know it, you have accomplished everything on your list.

Try to reward yourself after finishing your tasks. It will serve as a booster to go on and start with the next. Nothing is like the anticipation of finishing a task to get a reward in return. These rewards can also serve as the diversion you need after the hard work.

Make every second count: Identify and use your spare time. There are always times when you actually don't do anything constructive, even during a very busy day. Such time spots can be utilized if identified and planned for less serious works.

For example, in the process of resting, why not look over some notes just to familiarize yourself with them. You do not have to memorize or understand deeper, just scan through. In the process of scanning, your mind absorbs the details to be recovered later on.

Notes should be reviewed everyday: Keep aside some time every day for reviewing notes. When you look at your notes everyday, less time will be spent in studying when examination time comes. There will be no need to cram or memorize too many information at the shortest time.

Reviewing them regularly will make you prepare whenever your teachers decide to give you unexpected quizzes or tests. Some teachers test their students this way. They serve as a constant check up on how students are managing their subjects. The results of these quizzes give them an idea who is going through the notes and who is waiting for study.

Be a taskmaster: Figure out how much of your time is spent on studying and other school-related activities. Then check how much free time is left with you. You can budget your time better if you know how much time are being spent on a particular task.

It is also important that you give yourself some free time. So you will not find yourself losing your sanity altogether.

Do not waste time over nothing: Have you ever encountered a time when you used up all your time just thinking and driving yourself crazy with bad thoughts? When you have overcome that stage, think did you have any good result from it?

Why not just spend these times on more productive things? Even if you do not feel like doing anything demanding, you can always find a task that is less tiring. By starting that, you have to move a bit from the position you were in earlier.

Keep everything in perspective: In your goal setting stage, you may have included goals that you can achieve but are too difficult to do so in reality. While it is okay to set seemingly high goals, do not try to overdo them. Try to set realistic and reachable goals.

Don't try to be a perfectionist all the time. Especially, trying to have a perfect time management will only disappoint you in the end. Like all time management plans, these things should be open to change when the situation calls for it.

Nearly perfect goals are not that easy to achieve. Because you are also not perfect, do not expect things to turn out as you had anticipated.

Take enough rest so that your body can respond to urgent and high priority duty calls. You will need to slog in those final hours of exam preparation or project submission. Make sure that your body and mind stay with you in such crucial times by giving them sufficient time to cool down.

Time management is no magic. It's a skill which can be mastered by anyone who studies and practices it regularly. Once you see your goals getting achieved as per your planned schedule, you will feel more enthusiastic about improving your time management skills.

❑❑❑

5

TIME MANAGEMENT FOR COLLEGE STUDENTS

Do you remember anytime when you wanted to study, but you couldn't, because you didn't get enough time? In most probability, you will remember not only one, but many such instances.

One of the most important reasons for students in not getting enough time for studies is bad time management. Time management is nothing but making sure that you get to used important time slots for doing important things in your life.

Especially during college days, the skill of effectively managing time is far more desirable than any other skill you may have acquired. You will need to schedule your time for studies as you will be required to spend time on other activities as well.

After doing all the hard work when you finally make it to the college, it's natural that you are very excited. You want to make new friends, socialize with them and look forward to developing some serious relationships too.

Remember though, that entering into college is the easy part, the tough part would be finishing it in one piece. College can be fun and at the same time frustrating, especially when your professor is giving you a hard time.

Making it through college is not only about how smart you are. It is not about how much you scored in your college entrance exams and it is not all about studying. People need to socialize, it's part of their nature. College provides that but also requires you to study.

You see, you have to balance your time between studies and socializing. Some college students study their minds out but some of them do not make it through college because of stress. Some college students think of the university as one big party organization.

The students either do not know how important it is to socialize and some are just lazy to study or does not know how important education is.

You may be a genius but it is not the key to be successful in college. So what is the secret to get you through college?

Effective time management is the key.

Time must be balanced between many things. So that none of the priority tasks remain unattended. You will need to spend time in preparing for classes, studying for periodical exams, making presentations, attending seminars and participating into other college activities. Not to forget spending time with friends, and blocking enough time for rest at night.

Planning your time is not only important for studying but is also useful when you want to relieve the stress of being in college.

Here are some ways on how you can effectively manage your time.

Set goals. Know what you want to achieve and make it your priority. This can be anything, whether you want to achieve the goal in a day, a week, or a semester. Ask yourself what your academic goal is.

Making goals can make it easier for you to look straight ahead; instead of juggling subjects that you think is easy, this could be very stressful and often results in not achieving your goal.

If you have more than one goal, then it is a good idea to subdivide it into manageable pieces. List down what you want to achieve for one week and for another week.

Prioritize. Once you are determined on the goals you want to achieve, you need to prioritize the activities required by the goal. This will help you determine what particular task needs to be accomplished first and what tasks can be set aside in the mean time. To achieve your priorities more efficiently, try to mark deadlines in your calendar.

Time management planning is there for you to follow. Do not stray from it. The success of good time management lies in following it. Some college students get easily tempted by acquaintances to go to a party while they are studying.

They often think that they can put off the schedule until tomorrow. It often results in too much things to do the next day resulting in stress and frustration.

Make use of extra time. For example, instead of doing nothing in a class waiting for the professor, try to think of the last class assignment. If you are going to write an essay, use the time to think of a good topic for it.

There is another great way to manage your time. Simply break it down into small pieces and plan your activities for each small manageable piece. It will give you more control and let you manage your time at a finer level.

Always remember that sooner you finish any task, more time you will get to spend with your friends. That way you can make most of the time you have at hand.

There will be times when you will feel 24 hours are too less to finish a day's work. Don't get frustrated on such occasions. Simply refer to and practice your time management skills, and you will realize ways to beat the time rush.

Enjoy your college life to its fullest by managing your time effectively. It won't be far when you will successfully accomplish what you set out for!

Nobody can deny the fact that among any other institutions, students of any college or university are the ones, who are pressed most for time.

There are a lot of variety in today's college students. They come from different backgrounds, generation, race, gender and overall academic exposure. The days are gone when students used to get classified into just two categories—scholars and jerks. Now the students know what they want.

Lot of college students work on part time or full time jobs and attend college to seek higher positions in their careers. In addition to supporting their education, they have their own homes or apartments to maintain too.

In such teeming diversity of academic community, it is but important for University and colleges to stress out the need for time management skills. Efficiency in managing time is a necessity for every student down to the last busy one.

Each student, of course, has his or her own situation. Learning time management skills will assist them into making a system or method that is effective exclusively for each individual.

Managing and balancing time in every aspect of college life as he/she goes through is quite crucial for success. Many college students already learned the hard lesson that failure to manage their time well, will lead to negative outcome.

Here are some basic principles of time management which have proven effective through time:

- Avoid and fight rampant procrastination. Each of us has their own procrastination habits. Only by identifying and admitting that you succumb to procrastination is the way to break them.
- A time management calendar is needed where you must write all-important dates from birthdays and other social events to more important, never-should-be-forgotten classroom schedules.
- Set deadlines that you can achieve realistically.
- Identify your most productive time of the day where your level of energy is high. Once identified, set out to develop study habits.
- Of course, you must not let your priorities go awry. Every minute is precious for a college student. By knowing what your priority goals and activities are, you can have enough time for everything you have to do.
- No one has learned without committing a mistake.
- From time to time, learn to say No to family and friends
- Remember that you are not that perfect and learn to live with that fact, so as to avoid becoming a perfectionist.
- Always find time for rest and relaxation. This will allow you to unwind and free yourself from stress and pressure.

Here are some more time management tips for college students:

1. Just like any other large projects, homework or assignments should be broken down into manageable size. Instead of taking up large task at one go, you have smaller ones, to be finished at different schedules and at different manageable intervals.

2. Even if you are on campus, during intervals between classes, and few hours before the break, devour your lecture notes and books. Studying on campus is certainly a good habit to develop, especially since you are left with little time to study once you are in your job or attending to your kids/other commitments.

3. Reward yourself for coming up with efficient and effective time management methods as you mature in college.

4. Sleep is important for everyone. Do not deprive yourself from a well deserved sleep. Do not think that you waste your precious time in sleeping. You must stick to work even when it is your bedtime.

5. Once you feel pressure and stress closing in around you, seek the advice of administrators, or faculty you trust. A word of advice or a refreshing thought can be just the thing to lift back your spirits.

6. Socialize with peer students whenever you get a chance. Great ideas won't necessarily come out of your mind every time. Listen to others and tap any good habits or practices they follow.

Busy persons must always take time to properly schedule their time in order to maximize each precious minute as best as possible. College students must also know how to effectively schedule their time.

Working out a practically feasible schedule is quite a challenge. Just make sure that you do not have conflicting activities everyday. Take note of each important date or hour for everything you do.

Do not worry about having little time for yourself. Once you have completed your assignments and study, you will soon have more time for other responsibilities and tasks. Figure out a way to squeeze into your busy schedule precious few hours or minutes for your family, friends, and yourself.

Managing time is like juggling with glass balls. You need to know which ball to leave bouncing and which ball to pick up so that none of the balls fall on the ground.

Remember, more you pursue your time management habits, more will be the chances of success in your academic life. So go for it!

❑❑❑

6

CALENDAR TIME MANAGEMENT

So, you finally did it! All the hard work in school has paid and you successfully made it to college. That day is not too far when you will complete the college education and land into the career of your dreams!

But hold on, It's not as easy as it seems from outside. The challenges now are far more severe and you will see them coming from everywhere. One of the major difficulties is in maintaining sufficient funds in your bank account so as to support your tuitions, books and other necessary expenses. Part time jobs can provide some support, but it will be at the expense of your valuable study time.

Talking about your study time, it will not only be taken up by the job but by other important things also. You have to take care of many other activities which are part of your college education, such as organizing and participating in events, seminars and presentations. Socializing with new friends and attending parties will be on your list too.

Wondering how to balance your time? Don't worry; all you need to do is work on your time management skills and draw up a calendar for managing your time. The calendar of activities will help you adjust all your time so that you won't miss any event and still get enough time for your studies.

More and more Universities and Colleges are aware of the fact that college students have to work in order to survive and finance their college education. Because of this insight, these schools adjust their class schedules to meet every student's needs.

However, administrators and advisors in the office find a hard time in scheduling and managing classes for working college students. This is because there are too many people to schedule and manage and few people to draw up the class schedules.

College students who practice effective time management strategies can be of big help. You can assist the college administrators in drawing up class schedules that are effective for working students. Professionals at college need your definite schedules so that they can draw up a fair enough class schedules.

You can work out an efficient schedule by yourself, which takes into consideration your studies, and part time job schedules.

Here is a great method of setting up your calendar for time management:

1. First, you must have a semester calendar. Universities and other colleges provide students with blank semester calendars. You can obtain one through online or create one according to your own liking.

2. In the semester calendars, enter your class schedules, project due dates, registration dates and other important dates. These important dates may come from your class syllabi and the school timetables provided in their brochures and announcements. Enter each date as you find them into your semester calendar.

Set up your own due dates for each phase of a big project, like term papers and projects. You can also add personal commitments to social and personal events. Maintaining a semester calendar as your time management method will help you plan before a given schedule. This way, you will avoid last minute disasters.

3. You can also set up a weekly planner. Weekly planners are provided by institutions you can obtain them online or get them at the registration office during enrolment. If you want to, you can also buy or create your own.

Weekly planners are particularly useful when you need to plan and manage short-term deadlines such as weekly assignments or class schedules or assembly and practice sessions. Your preparation time for any class can also be entered in the calendar. If you are not sure of how much time you will need for reviewing topics taught in class, have a rule of thumb to block two hours of study time for each hour of a lecture.

Plan your regular time off from work and school. Enter bed and wake up times in your planner. Meanwhile, for projects, exams and other personal commitments, leave off blank slots.

4. Its important that you review and tally out your planner and semester calendar on a regular basis. This will enable you to check out the things you have accomplished for that week and adjust time for the pending and new activities for the week.

Incorporating these, other commitments can be done by placing them in the blank time schedule you have on your weekly planner. Then add new items you are committed to for the incoming week. Enter new things and schedules as new commitments and engagements come up.

You can check weekly planner before affirming to a commitment or engagement. If you find you have a previous entry on the said date and time, then it is best to turn down the invitation early on.

5. Every night create a daily 'action list' for the following day. Use your weekly and semester calendar to do this. You can even put in categories to set your priorities straight.

Your calendar for time management is an important tool to help you survive through difficult situations in your college life. Making a calendar and following it honestly will not only bring good results, but will also make you a more organized and systematic person, in overall.

❑❑❑

7

TIME MANAGEMENT TIPS

It's a miserable life for students. Regular weekly exams, recitations, different types of quizzes, homework and the load of projects cause a lot of stress to the students.

Life gets busy each and everyday. Getting enough of sleep is very crucial. Being a student also means picnics, cookouts, sports events, hanging out with friends and sometimes a job. So many things to do, and there is so little time.

One of the most important aspects in the life of an aspiring student is time management. When a student learns to manage his time, he not only learns to use his time wisely, but also understands the importance of every second.

Time management will give a student proper steps and ideas on how to schedule their time effectively. Besides that, proper time management can also teach a student to estimate how much time can be used in a certain activity. In their future lives, it helps them planning for things and work accordingly.

Most of the time, a student should have an accurate evaluation of their time. By doing this, the student can be able to keep track of their activities. It is a vital aspect for the students to have enough time to prepare for all of their subjects and their extra-curricular activities.

Mostly students are having enough time in the day to get everything done. But most of them are always late to go to their classes.

To make things more understandable, here are some tips for taking control of time and organizing some basics in life.

Plan your tasks: A 'to-do' list is an effective method of planning your daily tasks and deciding their priorities. Putting tasks, responsibilities and goals in writing are very important. The activities must be ranked from top priority to the lesser priority. This way, what needs to be done right away is prioritized.

Make use of spare time intelligently: Every tick of the clock hand is important. A minute lost is gone forever. Never waste a single minute doing something unproductive. For example, while on the bus read something. Alternatively, why not try reviewing some of your notes while on recess or a free period. Make use of your free time always, even if a project is not due yet, you can do it ahead if you have idle time, and you'll never know when a lot of activities can prevent you from doing so in the future.

Don't be afraid to use the word no—especially to your friends: It is very important to say no sometimes. For instance, a friend asks you to watch a concert on a school night. This could be time spent studying. Also, a concert can go on until the wee hours of the morning, you will feel sleepy and thus not fit for learning the next day. Always take the right decision. Always set your long-term and short-term priorities in mind. Remember that there is always the right time and place for everything.

Find the precise time for both work and studies: According to some studies, students can perform well in his studies more efficiently if they figured out their allotted time for work. For instance, if a student loves math during early morning better than afternoon, he should work it during that time.

Sleep well: If you do not take enough rest, you will not be able to perform your planned tasks as per schedule. Having a short rest can also give extra stress to the body making the task more difficult. With enough sleep, you can do your daily activities with a refreshed mind, allowing you to finish them faster saving more time.

Be the best 'task holder master': It is very important to shape out how much free time each week has. Giving oneself an allotted time management and activity planning can settle all time-consuming activities.

Do not waste time in worrying: Just relax and have peace of mind. Most of the students spend their time worrying doing nothing. It is not worthy. Instead of worrying and agonizing over something, find a solution and take the action right away. Never procrastinate.

Be optimistic: You must have a very positive point of view in whatever you do. Too much of speculation of problems will give you stress and degrade your quality of work.

Be flexible: No matter how much you plan in advance, there will always be times when you will need to adjust your calendar as per the needs of the hour. Also, you should understand that not all planned tasks will be met every time. Be prepared to adjust your schedules accordingly.

You can be a better scheduled student if you use these tips to your advantage. Remember, only practicing the time management techniques can make a man and even a student perfect!

❑❑❑

8

TIME MANAGEMENT SKILLS

Do you remember if you understood the importance of time when you were a kid? You won't. Because for most of us actually understood the difference a balanced and well managed timetable can make to our lives in achieving our goals much later.

Time is that priceless resource which everyone gets in equal amounts. 24 hours per day for everyone. Then why do some people become more successful in life than the others? Their secret lies in utilizing this resource intelligently and with maximum effectiveness. To learn to use time effectively, the art of time management must be taught from early childhood.

Are you concerned about poor time management skills of your students? What are the obstacles which stop them from finishing their assignments in school? Time management is indeed a problem for students.

Usually, it is due to their hectic schedules and social obligations from their peers. There are still very few people who could master this skill of time management. However, it is a general need for everyone especially if you are aspiring to achieve something in school, work and other personal endeavours.

There are many things which students need to take care of while studying. Attending classes in school as per schedule, completing homework assignments and executing school projects are just a few of the tasks that students need to manage. Given the fact that students are unaware of managing their time, it becomes very difficult for them to accomplish so many things, and sometimes they even fail.

Don't feel bad, as this is not the end of everything. What is necessary now is to re-evaluate how they have been coming up with their daily activities and try to modify them.

The students cannot do it by themselves. There is a need for somebody to teach and guide them. Apart from the regular class schedule, there are some activities for time management, which are integrated to the subject itself.

For this, make the students work in teams for two minutes so as to see the time monsters (time wasters) on a sheet of paper. Besides this, they will learn the acronym **CHOICE**.

Compare all your activities you would like to achieve.

How you will be affected by your choice later on.

Order all your priorities in life.

Inscribe in your planner your desired schedule.

Carry out whatever desired plan you have formulated.

Enjoy every moment of your life as you manage your time.

There are some questions for discussion, for example, the meaning of the word 'procrastination'. Some tips for time management are also provided according to the category you belong to.

We have several essential principles of Time Management which students can use.

- List down all the things you are supposed to do everyday.
- You should know what the most conducive time for you to study is.
- The difficult subjects must be studied first.
- Make use of your spare time.
- There should be proper distribution of learning and practice.
- The surroundings must be favourable for studying.
- Do not be afraid to say no to somebody if it affects your schedule.
- You should combine some activities to save time.
- Allot some time for relaxation and entertainment.
- You should have the required number of hours for sleeping and eat your food properly.

- You should know your body clock so as to identify the best time for you to work.
- Make it a habit to review your notes daily.
- You should inform your friends about your schedule in order to avoid distractions.
- Always be a taskmaster as you schedule your activities properly.
- Do not waste your time by worrying about something that you are expected to be doing, just do it.
- You should always keep things in their proper perspective.
- You can entrust a responsibility when it is proper.
- Relax and be calm always.
- Avoid being a perfectionist.
- You are supposed to question everything that is included in your schedule.
- Be a fast reader and be selective with what you read.

Make use of a calendar.

If students have a lot of time at their disposal, ask them to split it into small fractions and plan activities for each fraction, rather than scheduling one large task for the whole empty time slot. This gives better control over time. Also, no one likes to work on the same thing for hours together. It's always better to switch between tasks and keep the interest alive.

All these tips and guidelines will help you to teach students the importance of time. When your students will see their performances have improved due to better time management, you can be rest assured that they will practice these techniques for the rest of their lives.

❑❑❑

9

GROUP STUDY

Many teachers/professors agree that group study enhances students' performances, both in class discussions, as well as on tests.

Why does it work? Group study pays off because it brings about changes in two ways: firstly, it forces students to alter their old ways of thinking and secondly, it changes their less effective patterns of behaviour.

In a group environment, students are less likely to procrastinate. After all, it's easy to put off an assignment when you only have yourself to answer to, isn't it? But when you know that you have a whole group of people counting on you, you'll be more likely to get the job done.

Group study also encourages students to explain things aloud. By speaking to and listening to others, students often improve on recall ability, or ability to remember information on test day.

Students who study with others are also forced to become more organized. Once you learn to date and label your notes, you'll see that organized notes make much more sense at the end of the week than the jumbled, mix and match variety.

One more great benefit of group discussion is that many perspectives improve your chances of anticipating test questions. Group members will always bring up ideas and thoughts you'd never considered. The various views are sure to pay off on test day!

Finally, you'll likely find that the benefit of group study reaches far beyond the good results on test day. It will build self-confidence that you can use for the rest of your life. Speaking to small groups will prepare students for speaking to larger groups in the future—or more official groups such as college admission panels or hiring boards.

So go ahead and start building a group of like-minded students who share your goals for success. Be sure to develop a set of study rules to establish the 'where's' and 'how's' and stick by them. The results will show on report card day!

HOW TO FORM A STUDY GROUP ?

Imagine you're competing on a game show for a big prize, and you're challenged to come up with a mystery story, complete with clues, a good twist, and a surprise ending. You have half hour to complete your task, and you're pretty relaxed until you see your competitors. You're playing against a team of five students of your age, and they can collaborate on their work!

Chances are: most students would prefer to be in the team of five, because groups offer a variety of view points and strengths. No one person can do everything well, but a group of students working together can get great results in a shorter period of time.

In the above game show example, the group of five would be more likely to come up with better results at a faster pace because they would probably be benefitted from having a variety of skills and learning styles—like an analytical person, a good note taker, a lateral thinker, a person with great recall abilities, and a person who is able to explain things well.

STUDY GROUP TIPS

- If you decide to form a study group, you will need to establish some rules or guidelines to keep the group from losing enthusiasm.
- Limit the size of your group from six to three students for best results. Too many voices lead to confusion.
- If you have eight or more students who are interested in group study, simply form two groups and mix the membership from time to time. This will avoid hurt feelings and having a stronger and weaker group.
- Don't feel you have to limit yourself to study only with your friends. Pick smart people who do homework if your goal is to improve your grades.
- Establish a regular meeting place and time and encourage each other.
- Give your group a name. This will give the group a stronger identity and encourage participation.
- At your first meeting, encourage each member to talk about his/her strengths that will help the group.
- Take turns acting as group moderator, to keep the conversation on topic. The moderator should speak up if the conversation drifts too far from assignments.
- Predict test questions and quiz each other.
- Create a code word or prize for good ideas. Everyone likes to receive a pat on the back. Come up with a special word or small reward to congratulate group members when they come up with a right answer.
- Come up with a friendly word for members who are slacking off. Use it as a warning to encourage them to pull their weight!

❑ ❑ ❑

10

DEVELOP A STUDY GROUP

Your success may depend on it! It is a small investment of time and effort that will significantly increase your study efficiency and improve your grades. In college or school, teachers expect you to read and remember material from several textbooks. Without an effective and efficient study group, excelling would be very difficult for students.

Form your team: Find at least three classmates for the team. The team's task is to divide reading assignments by chapter. Each person creates an outline of his assigned chapters to share with other group members. As long as members do quality outlines, they may continue in the group and share the outlines. With this method, it is possible for a group of five students to gather all the important information from an average textbook of about 20-25 chapters in about four hours.

Share class notes: Keep lecture notes to share regularly or to help out group members who may miss a class. Keeping and sharing notes help to ensure that you catch all of the important points of a lecture. Working with others for the benefit of your study group, you will develop supportive friendships for the challenging years ahead.

Build social support: Get together with others who share your interests, as in a sports team, religious group, a special interest group, or group of students who share with you in study. It is important to surround yourself with positive people for mutual support. You will find others who have had courses with the same teachers you have and who may be able to offer good advice about the class and for working with the teacher. In turn, you may be able to help others.

Building social connections for your group: So, what can you do if you're not in an organization? Create your own group. Begin by being friendly with others in class. Notice which of your classmates seem to be good listeners and which take notes. Find organized students sitting at or near the front. Believe it or not, researchers have found that students who choose to sit in the front are usually the highest achievers.

Develop group expectations and rules: Arrange your group to meet for lunch to discuss how your group will work, what the rules should be, and who will take which assignments. Set deadlines for submitting notes and outlines to the other members. Create an outline of the group's rules, assignments and deadlines and ensure that each person gets a copy.

Develop a communication plan: Set up a means of sharing information and keeping a sense of belonging for everyone. Create a phone list, a telephone tree, or an online group through your college or social networking servers such as Orkut or Youtube to communicate important information. Each has its unique advantages.

Plan for sharing information: Online groups offer the opportunity to upload information, share links, and send digital copies of handouts from class or articles assigned for reading by the teacher. Telephone contacts offer more immediate communication and the opportunity to ask questions for clarification.

Develop a telephone tree: In a phone tree, any messages that the group needs to hear are submitted to the starting person. That person is responsible for calling two specific people, who call two other specific people. This continues until the whole group is reached. Of course, email and online groups are another way to do this and to share notes and copies, as long as everyone has access to the Internet.

Improve your study skills: As you work with your group, encourage each other to continue improving your study skills and sharing successful tips with each other. Visit Instructional Strategies and Materials for tips on improving reading comprehension, preventing reading fatigue, using a planner, and other terrific homework helps.

❑❑❑

11

HOMEWORK IS IMPORTANT

Assigning homework serves various educational needs. It serves as an intellectual discipline, establishes study habits, eases time constraints on the amount of curricular material that can be covered in class, and supplements and reinforces work done in school. In addition, it fosters student's initiative, independence, and responsibility and brings home and school closer.

Homework is defined as out-of-class tasks assigned to students as an extension or elaboration of classroom work. There are three types of homework: practice, preparation, and extension.

Practice assignments reinforce newly acquired skills. For example, students who have just learned a new method of solving a mathematical problem should be given sample problems to complete their own. Preparation assignments help students to be ready for activities that will occur in the classroom. Students may, for example, be required to do background research on a topic to be discussed later in class. Extension assignments are frequently long-term continuing projects that parallel class-work. Students must apply previous learning to complete these assignments, which include science fair projects and term papers.

Research in the last decade has begun to focus on the relationship between homework and student achievement and has greatly strengthened the case for homework. Although there are mixed findings about whether homework actually increases students' academic achievement, many teachers and parents agree that homework develops students' initiative and responsibility and fulfills the expectations of students, parents, and the public. Studies generally have found homework assignments to be most helpful if they are carefully planned by the teachers and have direct meaning to students.

HOW CAN PARENTS GET INVOLVED?

- Share any concerns you may have regarding the amount or type of homework assigned with your child's teacher or principal.
- Encourage your child to take notes concerning homework assignments in case questions arise later at home.
- Provide a suitable study area and the necessary tools (for example, paper and books) to complete the homework assignments.
- Limit after-school activities to allow time for both homework and family activities.
- Monitor television viewing and establish a specific homework time.
- Plan a homework schedule with your child. Allow for free time when assignments are completed.
- Praise your child's efforts. If questions arise about the assignments, and your child asks for help, ask him or her questions or work through an example rather than simply providing the answer.
- Younger children need more parental assistance with homework than older children. Go over homework assignments with your child. Do several problems or questions together, then observe your child doing the next one or two.
- Ask your child's teachers about their homework policy and specific assignments.

How much homework is adequate for the students, the experts vary on this subject. But generally following schedule is perfect regarding the quantum of homework.

- From kindergarten to third grade, no more than 30 minutes per day.
- From fourth to sixth grade, 30 to 50 minutes per day.
- From seventh to twelfth grade, the recommended amount of time varies according to the type and number of subjects

a student is taking. In general, college-bound students receive lengthier and more involved homework than students preparing to enter the workforce immediately after graduation.

SLEEPY DURING HOMEWORK?

Studies suggest that teenagers often sacrifice their sleep when it comes to making choices about time management. The problem is that they need a lot more sleep than they probably get.

According to a study by sleep expert, teens should get more than nine hours of sleep every night. That's a great thought, but is it possible? Think about it—do you *ever* sleep that long?

Okay, maybe on the weekends. But very few teens receive sufficient sleep on school nights.

A study suggests biology might be the cause for sleep deprivation among teens. Their internal time clocks are just a little different during teenage years—and late nights and sleep-ins are a natural part of growing into adulthood.

Lack of sleep makes it more difficult for students to concentrate in school, especially during those early-morning classes.

STUDIES ABOUT SLEEP AND MEMORY

Our ability to remember is related to our ability to learn, and there have been many studies about sleep and its effects on memory, learning, and retention. These studies suggest that good sleep habits are essential for good study habits.

One study about learning languages shows that it is good to study right before going to sleep because "there is near-consensus that sleep promotes learning of certain types of perceptual memories." In other words, sleep helps students store memories to be retained and remembered the next day.

Another study shows that sleep strengthens memories so they become clear and resistant to interferences and distractions.

A study suggests that information becomes 'cemented' in our brains as we sleep.

These studies show that sleep is important, but they also suggest that it may be most helpful to study right before bed time.

AVOIDING SLEEP DEPRIVATION

So what can you do if you know you aren't getting enough sleep?

Turn off the TV at night: Some teens fall asleep with the TV on, and some are so used to the noise that they think they can't sleep without it. Not true! The TV noises and flashing lights will only keep you away from getting a sound sleep. If you can remember things you heard during your sleep, you're not sleeping well.

Try caffeine free drinks: Try reducing caffeine by switching to something healthier, like bottled water. Okay, okay, if that's too much to ask, at least try a caffeine-free version of your favourite drink.

Limit after-school activities: It's hard to do, but try to limit your extra-curricular activities. Sometimes you just have to make a hard choice and stick to it.

You may need to strike a balance between sparing time for homework and sleep and gaining valuable experience in an extra-curricular activity that will help your chances of getting into a good college. Know your priorities.

Don't think too hard right before bed time: If you have calculus homework, you might not want to put it off until night. It's harder to relax and get to sleep when your mind is stuck in the deep-thinking mode. It takes a while to unwind, so maybe you should tackle the hardest subject earlier.

Same for crazy video games: Video games may also cause your brain to enter the overdrive zone. If you play video games, don't do them just before you go to bed.

Turn off the cell phone: What's so important that it can't wait until next morning? Unless you have a really good reason—like your parents work at night and might need to reach you, turn it off and get some rest.

Keep track of time: Often, students have great intentions, but other tasks seem to keep them up late, often. That's because teens have to develop an understanding of time management and task completion. It's hard to put a timetable on things like running an errand or completing a science experiment.

Start keeping track of things you do routinely and the amount of time needed to do certain tasks. Then plan ahead so that you can get to bed on time.

Play music if you want, but not too loud: Many people play music at night. If it doesn't bother you, go ahead. Don't play it too loud, though, or it will disrupt your sleep.

Do you really need that after-school job? : This might be a really tough decision, too. Some students need to work so they can pay for car insurance or save for college. You'll just have to decide on your own, what's necessary and what's not.

❑❑❑

12

HELPING YOUR CHILD WITH HOMEWORK

Homework is an important part of a child's learning process, it is also a great way for parents to get involved and stay informed about what is being taught. The best way to ensure a productive learning experience while doing homework depends on the child. Being stuck at a desk, in a quiet room, alone is not always the best way to learn.

When your child gets home from school, it is important to discuss their day and find out what homework they have been given. This allows you and your child to create a plan for getting the homework done.

Some children would rather jump right in and complete their homework rather than have it on their mind till afternoon. Others need a break from the day before they can delve into more schoolwork. Either scenario is fine, as long as there is a mutually agreed upon plan.

It is also important to give your child a healthy snack or dinner before they begin their homework. Hunger can be a major distraction, and kids are usually looking for an excuse to put off their homework. Eliminate the chance of this distraction by providing a healthy snack, preferably with protein. Good snacks include a piece of bread with butter, some carrots or a fruit smoothie. These snacks should keep their energy level up and keep them from feeling lethargic.

Next, decide on the best environment for your child to do their homework in. It could be at a desk in their room, at the kitchen table or in an office. Any area is fine as long as it is relatively free from distractions. Never allow your child to do homework with the television on. Many people prefer light background music, and studies have shown that it could be beneficial to thought, versus a room that is dead silent.

Before your child sits down to work, be sure that all the supplies they will need are readily available at the table. Also be sure that they have used the restroom and that they have a glass of water to drink. Avoiding these potential distractions will save your child's time once they begin their homework, as well as preventing breaks in their concentration level.

The amount of assistance you provide your child with their homework, again depends on the child. If you are concerned, consult their teacher for guidance on how much help they should be getting. In general, you should be available to answer questions but not hanging over their shoulder doing the work for them.

It is especially important to not overly assist your child on school projects. Oftentimes, parents end up making it their project and the child loses out on a valuable learning experience.

The most important things to remember when helping your child with their homework is to help them stay organized, provide a comfortable work environment and answer any questions they ask without being too involved.

❑❑❑

13

SAY GOODBYE TO IDIOT BOX

Teenagers who say their parents restrict their television viewing of certain programmes are likely to watch the restricted shows at friends' houses, a study suggests.

These teens also reported less positive attitudes toward their parents, according to the research.

Unfortunately, parents' good intentions in restricting television viewing may actually backfire and contribute to increase in watching more of the programmes they shouldn't have watched.

However, that doesn't mean parents are powerless to mould their teens' viewing habits. A research suggests that parents who discuss issues related to television with their older children – rather than just restrict viewing – are more likely to influence what their children watch. The key is to discuss without lecturing.

When parents talk to older children by asking questions and inviting dialogue, and don't talk to them in a condescending or threatening way, they are more likely to see positive outcomes.

In a recent study in the USA, 159 college students were asked questions about their television viewing habits and relationship with their parents during their high-school years. They were asked about their attitudes toward their parents, their attitudes toward violent and sexual content in TV shows and how often they watched TV shows containing violence and sex with their friends.

In addition, 138 parents (mostly mothers) of these students responded to a survey asking about their role in controlling their children's television viewing during high school.

Results showed that students whose parents restricted their access to objectionable television content had less positive feelings toward their parents than did other adolescents. These teens also reported viewing more of these objectionable television shows with friends than did other students.

The scenario in India is not alarming like the USA but tendency towards violence and sex is fast increasing in teens. Some recent untoward incidents are the evidence.

Adolescents sometimes resent being told what to do, and it can produce this forbidden fruit effect, in which the restricted shows seem even more appealing. They just end up watching the restricted shows at friends' houses.

But in another study researchers found methods parents can use to influence their children regarding inappropriate TV shows.

This study involved 103 children between the ages 5 to 12. The children viewed a five-minute edited episode of a television show in which three super-heroes were engaged in justified violence against enemies.

There were pauses between the programme, during which one of the researchers watching the show with the children made comments about what they were viewing. These comments are what are known as 'active mediation' and mimic what parents can do with children to get them to think about the programmes that they watch.

Immediately after viewing, the children completed a 15-minute questionnaire.

The results found that, among younger children, active mediation statements by the researchers discussing the violent nature of the programme did lead children to have less positive views toward the programme. These statements conveyed messages like "people in real life do not act like the people in the programme."

Among older children, though, statements about the violence of the programme led to a backlash by actually increasing the children's positive views of the programme.

However, when the researchers asked questions about the violence in the programme–rather than making statements–the older children showed a slight decrease in their positive orientation toward the show.

Older children and adolescents may see mediation statements–particularly negative ones--as condescending to them. But when parents raise questions and issues about the violence they see on television, older children pay attention. This seems to be more palatable to children who are developing their own ideas and who may resent hearing lectures.

❑❑❑

14

RESTRICT TV WATCHING

In a typical home, the TV is on for over 5- 7 hours every day. This startling information gives parents justifiable concern over the amount of time their teen spends in front of the TV. Watching television keeps teens away from other activities such as reading, socializing, and sports, which help in building skills and stay healthy. Even though some programmes are educational, these shows are not the ones teens tend to watch.

Research has shown continuously watching TV affects brain development. Too much television can contribute to poor grades, sleep problems, behaviour problems, and obesity. Teens spend too much time in front of the television and either don't do their homework or they don't pay attention to the subject matter while they are studying. This causes them to miss information and do poorly on tests.

Watching television till late night leads to insomnia and fatigue in teens, because they are staying up too late. This can also contribute to poor performance in school. It can also make your teens more irritable and difficult to get along with. They could become less interested in other activities like sports or cheerleading, because they are just too tired to participate.

Obesity is becoming an epidemic in India. Obese children are more likely to become obese adults. Television contributes to this problem because children aren't getting the exercise they need. They also tend to eat snacks more often while they are watching television, and research shows that eating while watching TV has an even worse effect of 'hooking' children to TV. It starts a bad habit and reinforces teen's dependence on TV.

Repeated exposure to TV violence makes teens less sensitive to its effects on victims and the suffering violence causes. Most violent acts go unpunished on television and are sometimes accompanied by humour.

HOW CAN YOU GET YOUR TEEN TO WATCH LESS TV?

Consider not allowing your teen to have a television in their room, because of the connection between too much TV and poor school performance and sleep problems. If your teen already has a television in their room, develop a way to restrict their watching time. For example, certain TV channels or programmes can be blocked through parental controls. You can also install a timer that cuts power to the television after a certain hour at night. This will keep teens away from watching shows that include violence or adult content, and keep them from watching TV too late in night.

Parents need to be diligent about the amount of TV their teen is watching. Talk to your teens about what programmes they would like to watch, and then develop a schedule where you can sit and watch the programme with them. Restrict the schedule to include only programmes and not blocks of time. This way your teens will be watching a half hour show rather than sitting in front of the TV before and after that show and watch what they wanted to watch.

Parents should not make watching TV a reward or punishment. It will only give undue importance to watching television. It's better to allow teens to watch certain programmes for a limited amount of time.

Parents should also separate important family activities from watching TV like having dinner. Make an effort to sit down at the kitchen table and eat dinner as a family without keeping the TV on. This will cut back the need for television and will lead to better communication in the family.

Parents can help their teens to maintain a diary for a few days in order to help them see how much time they are spending watching TV. They can also track what activities they may have missed while watching television. By noting the shows they watched, they can determine if they learned anything from watching those shows.

In the end, your teen is more likely to see how limited the rewards of viewing TV for long hours actually are.

Certain time or days of the week can also be designated as 'no television' time. Instead, these times can be designated for homework, reading, outdoor activity, or spending time with family. Family activities can include bike rides or game nights. When the entire family spends time together, parents can easily build and maintain bonds with their teens.

Parents can also encourage their teens to be more active in sports or other recreational activities, making hours in front of the TV less appealing to teens.

❑ ❑ ❑

15

SHUN JUNK FOOD

Talk to parents, dieticians, school counselors, even educationists, you will find that everyone is concerned about the fast growing dependence of teens on junk food.

If you think your child is naughty and half an hour of him/ her is enough to exhaust you, it might be wise to check the food you are giving your child. Junk food might just be the culprit.

Please note, though: there is a difference between junk food and fast food.

Sports nutritionists and child counselors say, "Fast food is food that is fast to cook. Idli is fast food and highly nutritious. Junk food harms the system with empty calories. It has no proteins and vitamins. For instance, aerated drinks fill your stomach with carbon dioxide and decay the food in your intestine. The high sugar content slows down the blood circulation in the brain.

The child feels full and is instantly energised. The energy then dissipates and the child is left lethargic in half an hour. S/he then wants more of the stuff, thus causing addiction."

WHAT JUNK FOOD REALLY IS?

- Junk food is a slang word for foods with limited nutritional value.
- To put it simply, foods high in salt, sugar, fat or calories and low nutrient content can be termed junk food.
- Salted snack foods, candy, gum, most desserts, fried fast food and carbonated beverages are some of the major junk foods.
- So if your child has fries at McDonald's or decides to wolf down sandwiches made at home, s/he is consuming junk food.

- Any over-cooked food or food that is cooked in high heat kills nutrition. What you consume then is fibre.
- All packed food contains preservatives. Most of them also contain food colouring. Both are harmful and often contain carcinogenic substances.
- When your child consumes foods like these, s/he could develop allergies like asthma and skin rashes.

A reputed Homeopath specialist advises parents to stop children from eating pre-packed snacks and drink aerated beverages when they come for prolonged allergies and asthma

attacks. "Half the time, they don't even require medication after that," he says.

PARENTS, HEED THIS!

Perhaps an easier way would be to educate adults and children on how to judge the food you eat.

1. While buying pre-packed, convenience food, check the list of ingredients and nutrition facts label found on the packages.

Keep an eye out for sugar, fat or salt as one of the first three ingredients. If any of these are listed high in the ingredients, consider that food to be very high in sugar, fat or salt.

The high sugar content in junk food causes tooth decay, increased tendency for blood clots, decreased levels of good cholesterol, increased levels of blood fat associated with diabetes, heart disease and childhood obesity.

2. The nutritional information on the label also registers the number of calories per serving, grams of fat, sodium, cholesterol, fibre and sugar content. This information will make you more cautious and select the foods to reduce your child's nutritional health risk.

3. Studies show that the colour of food affects us, too. The colours of some food are important. Some can calm you, while some act as anti-depressants. Some are stimulating, while others can be antiseptic.

Are all junk foods bad?

Not really, says dieticians. If you can balance junk food with a fruit or a whole vegetable, it is okay. Junk foods may have higher levels of fat, salt and sugar, but they still contain nutrients and can be considered a small part of a healthy diet.

A general 'rule of thumb' is to eat fresh, healthy foods about 90 per cent of the time, and indulge in junk foods not more than 10 per cent of the time.

❑❑❑

16

MAKE GOOD FRIENDS

How can we find true friendship in this often phony, temporary world? Friendship involves recognition or familiarity with another's personality. Friends often share likes and dislikes, interests, pursuits, and passion.

How can we recognize potential friendship? Signs include a mutual desire for companionship and perhaps a common bond. Beyond that, genuine friendship involves a shared sense of caring and concern, a desire to see one another grow and develop, and a hope for each other to succeed in all aspects of life. True friendship involves action: doing something for someone else while expecting nothing in return; sharing thoughts and feelings without fear of judgment or negative criticism.

We all have friends. A lot gets talked on the subject of friendship. Everyone wants a true friend, and many of us believe that we have a friend who can be called a true friend. What kind of relations do friends share? When can we call a friend a true friend, and when can our friends take us as their true friend. After a romantic relationship, friendships are the most important relationships we can have. Though all of us have family and distant family, most of us rely on friends for advice, comfort and inspiration. How do we define a relation that can be called as one of true friendships?

The very first sign of a very good friend, not necessarily a true friend is that we are not worried about courtesies. You will call your friend at any hour and talk without any thought of time in your mind. Similarly, whenever you need support, you will call a very good friend and ask him/her to help you out. They expect the same from you. Another important trait of such relations is that we are not much worried about exposing ourselves. We speak about everything in our mind without worrying about what our friends will think. We are sure that they will take our talk in the spirit it was made. We are unguarded and open with friends in our talk.

A true friend is a little more than a very good friend. He will support you even if it hurts his/her own interest. A true friend will understand your motives and needs and will be with you without any analysis or criticism. A true friend will come forward to help without any request and be with us in need without showing it or expecting anything in return. With a true friend, you can be sure that you will get help to the extent possible by him/her. Nothing will remain unturned. A mother is a true friend of her children. If we share such relations with an adult we can say that we are true friends.

A true friend makes no excuses of having work or appointments or anything but will be with you whenever you need him/her. In your hour of desperation, a true friend will support you even if the whole world opposes you. A true friend is not an opportunist. A true friend means to have someone who is like mother, as I said earlier. Instead of having hundreds of good friends, if you have a true friend, treat yourself lucky. If you can also become a true friend of someone, you will be blessed, because it is much easier for all of us to expect but very difficult to give. Be a true friend yourself first.

Peer relationships are very important to teens.

1. Friendships provide teens with opportunities to develop conflict resolution skills. Teens can learn how to end a fight and still remain friends.

2. Friends provide fun and excitement for teens through companionship and recreation.

3. Friends also give advice to one another. Teens talk through lots of issues and problems with their friends.

4. Loyalty is a valued trait in friendship. Teens are looking for loyal allies that can help them out at school or in their own neighborhood.

5. Friendships also provide stability during times of stress or transition. It is helpful to teens to have a friend who is going through the same situations and can ease the anxieties of the times.

What happens when youth don't have friends? Teens without friends tend to be more lonely and unhappy. They tend to have lower levels of academic achievement and lower self esteem. As they get older, they are more apt to drop out of school and to get involved in delinquent activities.

Friendships change with passing time.

- Teens tend to spend more time with their peers.
- They are also more mobile than when younger so more time is spent with peers without parental supervision.
- During the teen years, there will be increased contact with opposite-sex peers.
- In the early teen years, often small groups of friends or cliques are formed which help to boost their confidence and give them a sense of identity.

Another feature of the teen years is the emergence of crowds. These are large groups of teens who gather together because they have characteristics that identify them with a particular crowd. Teens use crowds to figure out who to associate with. Crowds help teens to sort peers into groups of people they would like to spend time with and those they wouldn't. Through crowds and cliques, teens show other people who they are.

As parents, it is important to encourage friendships among teens. However, it is vital to know who your teen's friends are and to communicate openly about changes in peer relationships and friendships with your teens.

❑❑❑

17

CONFIDENCE BUILDING TECHNIQUES

Self-confidence is extremely important in almost every aspect of our lives, yet so many people struggle to find it. Sadly, this can be a vicious circle: People who lack self-confidence can find it difficult to become successful. After all, would you instinctively want to back a project that was being pitched by someone who was nervous, fumbling and overly apologetic?

On the other hand, you might be persuaded by someone who spoke clearly, who held their head high, who answered questions assuredly, and who readily admitted when he/she did not know something.

Self-confident people inspire confidence in others: their audience, peers, bosses, customers, and friends. Gaining the confidence of others is one of the key ways in which a self-confident person finds success.

YOUR TWO MINDS

Your mind is actually composed of two distinct parts: Conscious and Subconscious.

The Left Brain–Your Conscious Mind : The left hemisphere of the brain deals with logical sequences, numeric calculations, words and their meanings, and speech. The left brain makes no excuses. It sees only the details; it cannot see beyond the immediate facts. It knows only what is going on now and demands those things to be in the proper order. It is scientific in approach and controls all rational conscious thought.

The Right Brain–Your Subconscious Mind : Your right brain deals with whole pictures, images, faces in a crowd, putting puzzles together, creative thinking, intuition, and musical and artistic ability. The right brain thinks in terms of the whole picture rather than focusing on separate details. It works out the meaning or significance of details even though you may not consciously be dwelling on them.

Using Left-Right Brain Combination to Change Your Behaviour : Think of your left brain as providing the "input," or information that has to be processed in your mind. Think of the right brain as the natural creative computer designed to process that information in order to come up with solutions for specific situations or problems. Your left brain tells your right brain what the facts are and what the objective is. YOUR RIGHT BRAIN EXAMINES THE FACTS AND WORKS OUT THE WAY TO ACHIEVE THE OBJECTIVE.

Decide what you want to do, and specify the changes necessary to achieve that end. Once you set the programme in motion by determining your goal, your right brain will automatically prompt you to make whatever decisions are necessary to reach that goal. Use visualization techniques described below.

NEGATIVE THINKING VERSUS POSITIVE THINKING

Your mind will go back and forth playing devil's advocate with you. Instead of thinking that you may not be able to do what is necessary to complete your goal, believe you will achieve your goal. Wish it, believe it, run a movie of it in your mind.

EVERY TIME YOU MAKE A STATEMENT YOUR SUBCINSCIOUS MIND (RIGHT BRAIN) REGISTERS IT AS A FACT. When you say out loud, "I can't," "I won't," "It's impossible," "I'm so clumsy," "I'm stupid," etc., your subconscious mind believes you and the task at hand becomes more difficult.

Catch yourself when you make a negative statement about yourself, and immediately change it into a positive one. Instead of accepting such thoughts and thus subconsciously allowing yourself to anticipate and welcome defeat, resolve to detect negative thoughts as soon as they begin to surface, and then repel them with immediate counter instructions.

If you force yourself to restate your negative thoughts into positive ones, you will have added another helper to your inner support network.

Instead of saying, I cannot do it, say that I will do better this time. Your right brain will consider that statement as a fact and do what is necessary to achieve that goal.

VISUALISATION

Your first goal is to get a mental picture of the behaviour, skill, attribute etc you wish to have.

Visualise success. DO NOT LET NEGATIVE THOUGHTS IN. The negative thoughts come from the logical, critical left brain. Control your brain input. Instruct yourself to do as you say. In your mind's eye, visualise success. Imagine what it feels like to obtain that success, savour the taste. Revel in the feeling of accomplishment. Never, never visualise failure. As you practice and create in your mind the images of what you want to happen, your body gets the message to make the condition happen.

Imagine the sights, sounds, smells and feelings of success. Use all of the senses to help reinforce the image of success. Spend some time relishing the whole gambit of feelings that accrue from success. . As you practice and create in your mind the images of what you want to achieve, the mind gets the message to achieve that goal.

PROGRESSIVE DESENSITISATION

Do not fight nervousness at a time when the fear is the greatest. Break it down into manageable portions.

If sitting for examinations is terrifying, imagine walking to the bus in the morning of an exam.

Get conditioned to the fear by just imagining the experience. Keep repeating this visualization. Then, imagine going to the exam room.

Again, do this until the fear is sustainable. Imagine opening the door to the exam room, sitting at the examination table, the wait before perusal time commences, opening the examination paper and reading the first question. Finally, imagine answering a question. In each visualization, you are becoming more desensitised to the experience of sitting for the examinations. You will have tempered yourself to the experience in manageable portions.

Repeat the above-mentioned process until you have overcome the terror of sitting for examinations.

There will always be some nervous energy in the examination hall, but the feelings of terror will be controlled.

❑❑❑

18

BOOST YOUR SELF CONFIDENCE

You feel anxious mingling at a party wondering if anyone will talk to you or if you will say anything engaging. You repeatedly check your appearance in the mirror. Perhaps, you failed at something you worked on and feel inadequate. You might even feel that you have been victimized and are not responsible for failure. All these symptoms share a common denominator: you are lacking self-confidence. Ironically being told that you lack self-confidence does not make you feel better about yourself!

Most daily stressors gnaw at the root of self-esteem. Filling your thoughts with perceived enemies and old conflicts drain your spirit and sap your creative joy. However, no one can trivialize you, label you, or crush your convictions if you have a fundamental sense of who you are; if you see yourself as a separate identity.

As you develop your focus and energy conservation techniques, you should find yourself becoming more self-confident in any given situation. It's inevitable that as you gain control over your thoughts and actions, you become more self-assured, simply because you know yourself better, and you can now control your own reactions.

This is an especially important skill to have when you are dealing with others. It doesn't matter what the situation is–whether you're dealing with classmates, teachers, or even your parents–the more self-confident you appear to the people you are dealing with, the more confident they will feel dealing with you. And the more confident others are in your abilities, the more confident you will feel within yourself.

How do you generate confidence and keep it going? Although others can often take it away, no one can hand it to you. It requires a leap of faith in yourself believing that if you work hard, are persistent, and connect with positive people, you will reap the rewards.

Here is how to take the first step. The secret to getting ahead is given below:

- Write down your goals to objectify and specify them. Often, we don't really think until we write.
- Express who you are by letting your inner self out! Dress the way you want and put on less make-up. You don't need a cover-up. Wear what is comfortable and makes you feel good.
- Close your eyes and visualise the successful outcome. Believe that things will work out. See yourself successfully completing the task, the steps in your mind, so that you become proficient. The less effort, the more proficient you will become.
- Shoo away the bullies in your mind like: can't, shouldn't which will ultimately lead to failure. Nothing is impossible to a willing mind.
- Find friends who will serve as your coach to inspire you to victory. You need a nurturing environment to grow. Imagine a sports team whose coach told them that they were not good and would lose. Ultimately the team would lose.
- If you fail, then assume responsibility. Learn from your mistakes and don't blame anyone else because then you give away your power. Victims are helpless. Don't let anger control you and defeat you.
- You don't have to excel at everything. Find something you do well and build on it. Let that something be your identifying success.
- Become so strong inside that you do not have to demonstrate your power. It is a part of you, readily observable in your stance with shoulders back, heart open and head erect.

❑❑❑

19

21 CONFIDENCE BOOSTERS TIPS

1. Groom yourself. This seems like such an obvious one, but it's amazing how much of difference a shower and a shave can make in determining your self-confidence and self-image. There have been days when I turned my mood around completely with this one little thing.

2. Dress nicely. A corollary of the first item above...if you dress nicely, you'll feel good about yourself. You'll feel successful and presentable and ready to tackle the world. Now, dressing nicely means something different for everyone...it doesn't necessarily mean wearing a costly or branded outfit, but could mean casual clothes that are nice looking and presentable.

3. Photoshop your self-image. Our self-image means so much to us, more than we often realize. We have a mental picture of ourselves, and it determines how confident we are in ourselves. But this picture isn't fixed and immutable. You can change it. Use your mental Photo shopping skills, and work on your self-image. If it's not a very good one, change it. Figure out why you see yourself that way, and find a way to fix it.

4. Get to know yourself. When going into battle, the wisest General learns to know his enemy very, very well. You can't defeat the enemy without knowing him. And when you're trying to overcome a negative self-image and replace it with self-confidence, your enemy is yourself. Get to know yourself well. Start listening to your thoughts. Start writing a journal about yourself, and the thoughts you have about yourself, and analyze why you have such negative thoughts. And then think about the good things and yourself, the things you can do well, the things you like. Start thinking about your limitations, and whether they're real limitations or just ones you've allowed to be placed there, artificially. Dig deep within yourself, and you'll come out with even greater self-confidence.

5. Act positive. More than just thinking positive, you have to put it into action. Action, actually, is the key to developing self-confidence. It's one thing to learn to think positive, but when you start acting on it, you change yourself, one action at a time. You are what you do, and so if you change what you do, you change what you are. Act in a positive way, take action instead of telling yourself: you can't, be positive. Talk to people in a positive way, put energy into your actions. You'll soon start to notice a difference.

6. Be kind and generous. Oh, so corny. If this is too corny for you, move on. But for the rest of you, know that being kind to others, and generous with yourself and your time and what you have, is a tremendous way to improve your self-image. You act in accordance with the Golden Rule, and you start to feel good about yourself, and to think that you are a good person. It does wonders for your self-confidence.

7. Get prepared. It's hard to be confident in yourself if you don't think you'll do well at something. Beat that feeling by preparing yourself as much as possible. Think about taking an exam: if you haven't studied, you won't have much confidence in your abilities to do well in the exam. But if you studied your butt off, you're prepared, and you'll be much more confident. Now think of life as your exam, and prepare yourself.

8. Know your principles and live them. What are the principles upon which your life is built? If you don't know, you will have trouble, because your life will feel directionless. Think about your principles...you might have them but perhaps you haven't given them much thought. Now think about whether you actually live these principles, or if you just believe in them but don't act on them.

9. Speak slowly. Such a simple thing, but it can have a big difference in how others perceive you. A person in authority, with authority, speaks slowly. It shows confidence. A person, who feels that he isn't worth listening to will speak quickly, because he doesn't want to keep others waiting for something not worthy of listening. Even if you don't feel the confidence in someone who speaks slowly, try doing it a few times. It will make you feel more confident. Of course, don't take it to an extreme, but just doesn't sound in hurry either.

10. Increase competence. How do you feel more competent? By becoming more competent. And how do you do that? By studying and practicing. Just do small bits at a time. If you want to be a more competent writer, for example, don't try to tackle the entire profession of writing all at once. Just begin to write more such as journal, blog, write short stories, do some freelance writing. The more you write, the better you'll be. Set aside 30 minutes a day to write, and the practice will increase your competence.

11. Set a small goal and achieve it. People often make the mistake of shooting for the moon, and when they fail, they get discouraged. Instead, shoot for something much more achievable. Set a goal you *know* you can achieve, and then achieve it. You'll feel good about that. Now set another small goal and achieve that. The more you achieve small goals, the better you'll be at it, and the better you'll feel. Soon you'll be setting bigger (but still achievable) goals and achieving those too.

12. Change a small habit. Not a big one, like quitting smoking. Just a small one, like writing things down. Or waking up 10 minutes earlier. Or drinking a glass of water when you wake up. Something small that you know you can do. Do it for a month. When you've accomplished it, you'll feel happy.

13. Focus on solutions. If you are a complainer, or focus on problems, change your focus now. Focusing on solutions instead of problems is one of the best things you can do for your confidence and your career. "I'm fat and lazy!" So how can you solve that? "But I can't motivate myself!" So how can you solve that? "But I have no energy!" So what's the solution?

14. Smile. Another trifle thing, but it works. We feel instantly better when we smile, and it helps us to be kinder to others as well. A little small thing that can have a chain reaction still it is not a bad investment of your time and energy either.

15. Volunteer. It's the holiday season right now...can you find the time to volunteer for a good cause, to spread some holiday cheer, to make the lives of others better? It'll be some of the best time you've ever spent, and an amazing side benefit is that you'll feel better about yourself, instantly.

16. Exercise. Exercise has been one of the most empowering activities and it makes you feel so much better about yourself. All you have to do is take a walk a few times a week, and you'll see benefits.

17. Empower yourself with knowledge. Empowering yourself, in general, is one of the best strategies for building self-confidence. You can do that in many ways, but one of the surest ways to empower yourself is through knowledge. This is along the same vein as building competence and getting prepared...by becoming more knowledgeable, you'll be more confident...and you become more knowledgeable by doing research and studying. The Internet is a great tool, of course, but so are the people around you, people who have done what you want, books, magazines, and educational institutions.

18. Do something you've been procrastinating on. What's on your to-do list that's been sitting there? Do it first in the morning, and get it out of the way. You'll feel great about yourself.

19. Get active. Doing something is almost always better than not doing anything. Of course, doing something could lead to mistakes... but mistakes are a part of life. It's how we learn. Without mistakes, we'd never get better. So don't worry about those. Just do something. Get off your butt and get active—physically, or actively by taking steps to accomplish something.

20. Work on small things. Trying to take on a huge project or task can be overwhelming, daunting and intimidating for anyone, even the best of us. Instead, learn to break off small chunks and work in bursts. Small little achievements make you feel good, and they add up to big achievements. Learn to work like this all the time, and soon you'll be a self-confident maniac.

21. Clear your desk. This might seem like a small, simple thing (then again, for some of you it might not be so small). But it has always worked wonders.

❑❑❑

20

THE 2 MINUTE CONFIDENCE BOOSTER

One of the key components to being self-confident is peace of mind. It's another reason why staying calm and relaxed is such an important part of mental concentration. When you have peace of mind, you will not feel timid, anxious, fearful, or any of the other negative emotions that can make you appear less than confident.

It helps to think in a spiritual sense. Think of yourself as a spark of the Divine. When you see yourself in this way, you can't help but feel more confident in yourself and your ability to accomplish whatever you set out to do.

For those times when you need a quick boost to your confidence levels, you can use this exercise:

The Two-Minute Confidence Booster

Stand in front of a mirror, and visualise your reflection as the person you will be interacting with. Centre your attention on keeping your head perfectly still. To help with this, you can use the visualization of your head being suspended by a string. This keeps your head and neck aligned, avoids building up tension in the neck area, and allows for an improved flow of energy throughout your body.

Focus on the thought that you are a person who inspires confidence.

Still standing before the mirror, practice taking deep breaths. See that there is plenty of fresh air in the room, and that you are literally feasting on it. Feel the fresh air filling up your body as you inhale, and as you exhale, feel all the tension and anxiety leaving your body.

You will find that as the fresh air permeates every cell in your body, any sense of nervousness or timidity will disappear,.and will be replaced with a sense of peace and power.

You can also use this affirmation to help: "Absolutely everything goes my way."

This is very helpful if you are unsure of the outcome of the meeting. such as an interview, appointment, first day in school/college, etc.

❑ ❑ ❑

21

REDUCE STUDY STRESS LEVEL

As educational requirements get more stringent at all levels of education, students everywhere experience considerable school-related stress. Here are some stress relief tips and tools that students can use to learn study skills, prepare for exams and minimize their stress levels to make learning easier, including an explanation of the importance of stress management, and resources to help you reduce the school-related stress.

Manage time wisely: It's important to give yourself plenty of time to work on your studies if you want to do well, and you can save yourself from a lot of stress if you plan ahead with good time management skills. Setting up a schedule for study, breaking up your studies into smaller chunks, and other time management skills are essential. Here are some more time management tips you may find helpful.

Get organized: Have a system for note-taking, keeping track of assignments, and other important papers. Being organized can bring you the peace of mind that comes from knowing where everything is, remembering deadlines and test dates, and clearing your mind of some of the mental clutter that disorganization brings. Keep a calendar, a schedule, and a filing system for your school assignments, and you'll find that it prevents a significant amount of stress!

Create a good study environment: Creating a soothing environment can reduce stress *and* help you learn. Aromatherapy, for example, is a known stress reliever, and peppermint-essential oil is said to wake up your brain. Playing classical music as you study can also soothe and help you to learn (unless you find it distracting). Here's more on finding a good study space.

Know your learning style: Did you know that we don't all learn in the same way? It's important to know whether you're a visual, kinesthetic or auditory learner, as you can tailor your study practices around your particular learning style and make success easier to attain.

Practice visualizations: Visualizations and imagery are proven stress management techniques. You can also reduce stress and improve test performance by imagining yourself achieving your goals. Take a few minutes each day and visualise, in detail, what you'd like to happen, whether it's giving a presentation without getting nervous, acing an exam, or something else that will support your success. Then work hard and make it happen!

Develop optimism: It's been proven that optimists—those who more easily shrug off failures and multiply successes—are healthier, less stressed, and more successful. You can develop the traits of optimism and harness these benefits for yourself, and do better in your studies as a result.

Get enough sleep: If you want your performance to be optimum you need to be well-rested. Researches show that those who are sleep-deprived have more trouble in learning and remembering and perform poorly. Work your schedule so you get enough sleep, or take power naps.

Use stress management techniques: Chronic stress can actually impair your ability to learn and remember facts as well, stress management is one of the most important—and most overlooked—school necessities. A regular stress management practice can reduce your overall stress level and help you to be prepared for whatever comes. This self test will help you choose wisely.

Learn study skills: Use some more specific study skills and techniques that can help you improve your performance. The more prepared you are, the less stressed you'll be!

❑❑❑

22

STRESS RELIEF RELAXATION TECHNIQUES

The body's natural relaxation response is a powerful antidote to stress. Relaxation techniques such as deep breathing, visualization, progressive muscle relaxation, meditation, and yoga can help you activate this relaxation response. When practiced regularly, these activities lead to a reduction in your everyday stress levels. What's more, they also serve a protective quality by teaching you how to stay calm and collected.

Whenever we encounter a stressful event, our bodies undergo a series of involuntary hormonal and biochemical changes. This automatic stress response, also called the *fight-or-flight reaction*, puts our bodies in alarm mode: heart rate speeds up, breath becomes shallow, muscles tense, and our digestive and immune systems temporarily shut down. The stress response is helpful in true emergency situations, but when it's activated on a frequent basis it puts strain on both mind and body.

No one can avoid all stress, but you can counteract it by learning how to evoke the *relaxation response,* a state of deep rest that is the polar opposite of the stress response. The relaxation response brings your system back into balance, reducing stress hormones, slowing down your muscles and organs, and increasing blood flow to the brain.

When the relaxation response is activated:

- Your heart rate decreases
- Breathing becomes slower and deeper
- Blood pressure drops or stabilizes
- Your muscles relax

In addition to its calming physical effects, research has shown that the relaxation response also increases energy and focus, combats illness, relieves aches and pains, heightens problem-solving abilities, and boosts motivation and productivity. Best of all, anyone can reap these benefits.

Many relaxation techniques can help you achieve the relaxation response. Those whose stress-busting benefits have been widely studied include deep breathing, progressive muscle relaxation, meditation, visualization and yoga.

Learning the basics of these relaxation techniques isn't difficult. But it takes practice to truly harness their stress-relieving power: daily practice, in fact. Most stress experts recommend setting aside at least 10 to 20 minutes a day for your relaxation practice. If you'd like to get even more stress relief, aim for 30 minutes to an hour.

Keep in mind that there is no single relaxation technique that is best. Many techniques are effective, but only when practiced regularly: so choose a relaxation technique or combination of techniques that resonates with you and fits your lifestyle.

The best way to start and maintain a daily stress relief practice is by incorporating it into your daily routine. Schedule a set time either once or twice a day for your relaxation practice. You may find that it's easier to stick with your practice if you do it first thing in the morning, before other tasks and responsibilities get in the way.

All you need to start a relaxation practice are:

- **A quiet environment** – Choose a secluded place in your home, office, garden, place of worship, or in the great outdoors where you can relax without distractions or interruptions.
- **A comfortable position** – Get comfortable, but avoid lying down as this may lead to you falling asleep. Sit up with your spine straight, either in a chair or on the floor. You can also try a cross-legged or lotus position.
- **A point of focus** – Pick a meaningful word or phrase and repeat it throughout your session. You may also focus on an object in your surroundings to enhance your concentration, or alternately, you can close your eyes.
- **A passive attitude** – Don't worry about distracting thoughts that go through your mind or about how well you're doing. If thoughts intrude during your relaxation session, don't fight them. Instead, gently turn your attention back to your point of focus.

You can either stick to this straight forward relaxation exercise, or branch out into other relaxation techniques. Keep in mind that traditional relaxation techniques aren't the only effective stress reducers. Spending time in nature, talking to a friend, listening to music, curling up with a good book, writing in a journal—anything that you find calming can relieve stress.

PROGRESSIVE MUSCLE RELAXATION

Progressive muscle relaxation is another effective and widely used strategy for relieving stress. It involves a two-step process in which you feel systematically tense and relax different muscle groups in the body.

With regular practice, progressive muscle relaxation gives you an intimate familiarity with what tension—as well as complete relaxation—feels like in different parts of the body. This awareness helps you spot and counteract the first signs of the muscular tension that accompanies stress. And as your body relaxes, so will your mind. You can combine deep breathing with progressive muscle relaxation for an additional level of relief from stress.

- Loosen your clothing, take off your shoes, and get comfortable.
- Take a few minutes to relax, breathing in and out in slow, deep breaths.
- When you're relaxed and ready to start, shift your attention to your right foot. Take a moment to focus on the way it feels.
- Slowly tense the muscles in your right foot, squeezing as tightly as you can. Hold for a count of 10.
- Relax your right foot. Focus on the tension flowing away and the way your foot feels as it becomes limp and loose.
- Stay in this relaxed state for a moment, breathing deeply and slowly.
- When you're ready, shift your attention to your left foot. Follow the same sequence of muscle tension and release.
- Move slowly up through your body—legs, abdomen, back, neck, face—contracting and relaxing the muscle groups as you go.

❑❑❑

23

MEDITATION FOR STRESS RELIEF

Meditation has a long history in religions such as Buddhism and Hinduism. And while it is still widely used as a spiritual practice, it is also a powerful stress reliever. Meditation focuses the mind's energy on a word, a sound, a symbol, a comforting image, or your own breathing. The goal is to produce a deep state of relaxation and tranquility while simultaneously enhancing mental focus. There are many types of meditation—secular and sacred—so regardless of religious affiliation or beliefs, you can harness its stress-busting benefits.

Meditation that cultivates *mindfulness* is particularly effective at reducing stress, as well as anxiety, depression, and other negative emotions. Mindfulness is the quality of being fully engaged in the present moment, without analyzing or otherwise 'over-thinking' the experience. Rather than worrying about the future or dwelling on the past, mindfulness meditation switches the focus to what's happening right now.

The goal of mindfulness meditation is to develop a non-judgmental, moment-to-moment awareness of what you're experiencing: random thoughts, your passing emotions, the sensations of your body, sensory input from your surroundings. However, mindfulness meditation is not equal to zoning out. It involves a challenging and balancing act between boredom and distraction. It takes effort to maintain your concentration and to bring it back to the present moment when your mind wanders or you start to drift off. But the very act of redirecting your attention is where the learning and growth occur.

With practice, mindfulness meditation teaches you to become acutely aware of your fluctuating emotions without reacting to them or letting negativity take over. For stress relief, try the following mindfulness techniques:

- **Body scan**: Body scanning cultivates mindfulness by focusing your attention on various parts of your body. Like progressive muscle relaxation, you start with your feet and work your way up. However, instead of tensing and relaxing your muscles, you simply focus on the way each part of your body feels without labeling the sensations as either "good" or "bad".
- **Walking meditation**: You don't have to be seated or still to meditate. In walking meditation, mindfulness involves being focused on the physicality of each step—the sensation of your feet touching the ground, the rhythm of your breath while moving, and feeling the wind against your face.
- **Mindful eating**: If you reach for food when you're under stress or gulp your meals down in a rush, try eating mindfully. Sit down at the table and focus your full attention on the meal (no TV, newspapers, or eating on the run). Eat slowly, taking the time to fully enjoy and concentrate on each bite.

❑❑❑

24

OVERCOME EXAM FEVER

Come exam time and students start getting anxious and spend sleepless nights worrying about the coming exams. Exams may be anxiety provoking for some people. Students may worry about an exam for days before it is to take place and/or during the exam, when tackling the examination they may experience negative thoughts and unpleasant physical symptoms which prevent them from performing to the best of their ability.

Students, Just Relax ! Need not Worry...It is wise to remember that exams are not here as punishment. Instead, they are a good way of testing to see how much information you have learned.

Examinations test a student's knowledge and understanding of a particular subject. They bring questions from an entire module together in a challenging environment. Whether you are taking the Board Exams or forthcoming Medical Entrance Test or appearing for any other Entrance Exam, Don't you worry. Just follow these simple tips to overcome exam fever.

Don't get over anxious: It never helps. Think of all the exams you have faced so far and how you have overcome your fears. Visualise the worst that can happen and then think positive.

Talk over your anxieties to your parents, friends etc. and get it out of your heart periodically. At the same time, talk about the subjects you are good in and the chapters you are well prepared in.

Gain confidence in subjects you know best: by completing the revision and writing notes, especially to a family member or answering mock tests. Make brief points to refer just before the exams.

Fix time and place: Make sure while studying disturbances don't bother you. Move away from that place when you need to take breaks. Take them frequently by structuring your time schedule.

Every time you feel fresh, study the difficult or boring subjects first for a few minutes and then move on to easy ones.

Exercise and recreation are as important as studies and they help you concentrate better. Don't reduce your sleep drastically. Your body needs it.

Avoid repetitive reading: If you are unable to remember, break up the chapter into points and sub points and try and remember each sub point.

Do mock tests periodically, especially in difficult subjects. Rest, eat good food and freshen up: especially on the morning of your exam. It is a better way to face them than last minute cramming.

On the day of the exam: Relax. Remember God is In-charge. Reduce stress, sleep well, eat well and leave early for examination centre. Do discuss with your friends what you have prepared and what you have not. Have confidence, you will do well. Believe in yourself.

❑❑❑

25

DON'T FORGET RECREATION

There are ways through which our knowledge can escape the boundaries set by syllabus. Here are a few ways to broaden your outlook:

Wonder who were your ancestors? How they got into the city or pursue a vocation? This may sound strange but it can be very interesting. Ask elders in the family about ancestors and how they got into the city or set up their vocation. You may get to hear interesting anecdotes that will clear out notions about a 'past society'. What's more, you can actually brush up your history skills once you get to know in which niche your family fit. Understanding the other strata of vocation in this context will be a fairly easy task. Another way to improve on your skills is by constantly learning through failures. A failure is merely the outcome of an action. Do not let failure deter you from your set goals. Learn from failures and avoid repeating mistakes. There are no better teachers than failure, so long as you do not let them depress you.

TURN TV WATCHING, A GAINFUL PASTIME

It is a battle that goes on in every home: Parents scolding the kids for watching too much TV and kids not responding to their parent's pleas. Try this. For every three programmes that you watch, write down a description of any one show. As it will be a task you set yourself. Thus you will find yourself inclined to do it. Involving your parents in this would be a good idea as they then might be more tolerant towards your TV viewing. Your language skills will improve and so will your power of observation and recall.

CHASE AWAY SWIMMING BLUES

If you are learning how to swim, several instructions will be given to you – limbs straight, head under water, breathe out through your mouth and so on. But for a beginner it seems impossible to do all this at the same time. Here is a tool to make the situation easy. Close your eyes and visualise yourself following the instructions that you have been given and then plunge in. You will find your performance better. Visualise yourself successfully reaching the other side before making each plunge and you can see all the instructions being effortlessly incorporated in your movements.

DON THE CHEF'S CAP

Don't we all appreciate something that is tasty and cooked to perfection? Well, all of us cannot turn into perfect cooks but then we should be at least self sufficient enough to have the capability to appease our hunger with a tolerantly tasty tidbit. It would be a good idea to spend some time with mom in the kitchen and pick up some rudimentary skills like fixing tea, coffee, milk with your favourite flavouring and if you are allowed to handle gadgets then maybe milkshakes. Knowing how to fix small snacks like sandwiches, instant noodles. And would it not be a treat for your mother if you can occasionally pamper her with a steaming cup of tea and some sandwiches?

TIME FOR HOBBIES

Love to pursue a hobby but do not find the time for it? Often you will find that you do have time at your disposal but are not able to think of something useful to do. As a result you fritter it away and before knowing it, you again have something important to do and that's it, the day is over. Well, try this.

- Fitting a hobby into your schedule should be done consciously and deliberately.
- Take a pragmatic look at your schedule and allocate a convenient time for your hobby. Say, Saturday morning 10 a.m.

- Do not lose heart if something else crops up. As a result of missing a scheduled activity you will find yourself remembering it the minute you have some free time. With practice you will get accustomed to thinking about your hobby every Saturday and then finding the time and energy to devote to it. It is just a matter of forming a new habit.

CREATE PUZZLES

Use your expertise with words to make your own word puzzles. Start off with some aimed at younger age group and then with practice, work your way up. A good way to start is to create a word grid in which the player has to search for words. You may start with an 8x8 grid and fill it up with words arranged horizontally, vertically or diagonally. Variations could be grids with words arranged only horizontally, or only vertically or only diagonally. Selections of words can be made as per a particular theme. Empty spaces can be filled up with a good assortment of alphabets designed to put the player off course.

DANCE, DRAW, PLAY...

Physical movements that involve timing and coordination encourage dendrite growth in the brain. And as the number of dendrites grows your brain can make more connections. This translates into efficient and flexible thinking, which in turn makes you more productive. So make time for activities like playing musical instruments, athletics, dance, drawing or any similar activity. As you pick up the new skill you will find your academic performance also being enhanced.

A SPECIAL WAY TO ANNOUNCE YOUR VISIT

You undoubtedly visit a lot of people during the vacations. At times some people are not home when you go over, or maybe there are some you meet whom you want to get in touch with again and vice-versa. In both cases, you usually leave behind your name and telephone number/address so that the person may get in touch with you. Make some colourful visiting cards, yes like the ones yon have seen adults use, but yours can be better and more colourful. Another trick to make this even more interesting is to use material that you have otherwise discarded like, cardboard and sheets of paper from blank pages of used notebooks and of course all the paints, colour pens and crayons left over from the year before.

Beware! When exam time is approaching it is trying to spend all your waking hours studying. Allow yourself to relax by giving yourself short breaks. Do something you really enjoy, this change of activity will give your mind the kind of 'rest' it needs. And then when you go back to your studies you will feel recharged and will be able to study better. Set yourself for achievable study related goals and treat yourself to these relaxation breaks after each goal is achieved. You will find your study sessions effortless and more productive. The treat at the end of the task will spur you on towards completing it.

❑❑❑

26

INCREASE YOUR READING SPEED

Speed reading helps you to read and understand text more quickly. It is an essential skill in any environment where you have to master large volumes of information quickly, as is the norm in fast-moving professional environments. And it's a key technique to learn if you suffer from 'Information Overload'.

The most important trick about speed reading is to know what information you want from a document before you start reading it: if you only want an outline of the issue that the document discusses, then you can skim the document quickly and extract only the essential facts. If you need to understand the real detail of the document, then you need to read it slowly enough to understand it fully.

TECHNICAL ISSUES

Even when you know how to ignore irrelevant issues, there are other technical improvements you can make to your reading style which will increase your reading speed.

Most people learn to read the way young children read—either letter-by-letter, or word-by-word. As an adult, this is probably not the way you read now - think about how your eye muscles are moving as you read this. You will probably find that you are fixing your eyes on one block of words, then moving your eyes to the next block of words, and so on. You are reading blocks of words at a time, not individual words one-by-one. You may also notice that you do not always go from one block to the next: sometimes you may move back to the previous block if you are unsure about something.

A skilled reader will read many words in each block. He or she will only dwell on each block for an instant, and will then move on. Only rarely will the reader's eyes skip back to a previous block of words. This reduces the amount of work that the reader's eyes have to do.

It also increases the volume of information that can be examined in a period of time.

A poor reader will become bogged down, spending a lot of time reading small blocks of words. He or she will skip back often, losing the flow and structure of the text and overall understanding of the subject. This irregular eye movement makes reading tiring. Poor readers tend to dislike reading, and may find it harder to concentrate and understand written information.

Speed reading aims to improve reading skills by:

- **Increasing the number of words in each block:** This needs a conscious effort. Try to expand the number of words that you read at a time: With practice, you'll find you read faster. You may also find that you can increase the number of words in each block by holding the text a little further from your eyes. The more words you can read in each block, the faster you will read!
- **Reducing fixation time:** The minimum length of time needed to read each block is probably only a half of a second. By pushing yourself to reduce the time you take, you will get better at picking up information quickly. Again, this is a matter of practice and confidence.

- **Reducing skip-back:** To reduce the number of times that your eyes skip back to the previous sentence, run a pointer along the line as you read. This could be a finger, a pen or a pencil. Your eyes will follow the tip of your pointer, smoothing the flow of your reading. The speed at which you read using this method will largely depend on the speed at which you move the pointer.

You will be able to increase your reading speed and a certain amount on your own by applying speed reading techniques.

By speed reading you can read information more quickly. You may also get a better understanding of it as you will hold more of it in short term memory.

To improve the speed of your reading, read more words in each block and reduce the length of time spent reading each block. Use a pointer to smooth the way your eyes move and reduce skip-back.

❑❑❑

27

READING WELL

As a student, it is important for you to buy relevant study material. Here are some tips that will help you buy the right books always and buy more with less.

Form a book pool: You don't have to add each book that you may need currently to your lifetime book collection. So why itch to own a copy? Form a book pool with some friends and buy books collectively. Keep them till you need and then sell them off to buy more relevant books. This will not only save money but also ensure that you don't collect books which is not required later.

Be sure of what you want: Have clarity on what you want the book to cover before you walk into a bookstore. Compare the contents of a few books to figure which one covers the relevant topics better before making the final decision.

Don't base your buying decision on the content page alone: Though it's fair to derive information on what the book comprises from the contents/index page, you still need to turn pages over to figure out how these content heads have been covered. Check for understandability of language, clarity of content, flow, depth required and so on. You can go through 4-5 topics at random to arrive at a decision.

Always be open to bargains: Ask your seniors if they have the books you are looking for. You might get a second hand copy from them at a less price. Also, always enquire at the bookstore for a second hand copy of the book you want, in usable condition. You anyway will want the book for a year so it's cool to grab a second hand copy and invest the saved money in another book.

Ask your instructors for guidance on what to buy: Teachers tend to know some of the best reference books on their subjects. So ask them for their referrals. If you have come across a book that you think is better than one they have recommended, do mention the name and the details to them for a second opinion. After all, they will be the one who will check your answer sheets so might as well study from the books they approve of.

Doing things effectively yet quickly has become a mandate in this world where time is less and work is more. Thus, the acquisition of rapid reading skills become important for students as it helps them to study more effectively in lesser time and also increases their power to assimilate and concentrate.

WHAT EXACTLY IS RAPID READING?

Reading that is faster than a person's normal rate of reading, in other words, reading that is accelerated is called rapid reading. Rapid reading is often used for specific purposes, as to locate essential information only, to get an overview of text, etc.

Rapid reading skills enable you to improve:

- Your reading ability so that you can find the information you need quickly and easily
- The skills for making notes so that the notes you make are clear, easy to understand and quick to review
- Your revision techniques so that you can retain information in your mind

KEY INSIGHT

The most significant secret of rapid reading is to know what information you want from a particular chapter before you start reading it. If you want only an outline of what the chapter consists of, then you can skim through the chapter quickly by running your eyes through the chapter with extreme concentration and extract only the essential facts. If you need to understand and assimilate the chapter in detail then you must read it slowly enough to absorb all nuances and concepts well and yet not too slowly as that will give space to your mind to wander.

TIPS

Here are some helpful tips and tricks that will enable you to master rapid reading skills:

Increase the number of words to be read in one go: Yes! Expanding the number of words that you read at a time will take a conscious effort from your end but it will help you in achieving the larger goal. With practice, you will be able to read faster. Holding the text a little further from your eyes also significantly helps in increasing the number of words in each block. The more words you can read in each block, the faster you will read!

Reducing fixation time: The minimum length of time needed to read each block is probably only a quarter of a second. But most of us, when reading at peace or luxuriously, take much longer. By pushing yourself to reduce the time you take to read one block, you will get better at picking up information quickly. Again, this will largely improve with practice and confidence.

Skip obstacles and come back to them later: While reading a passage, if you don't get a word's meaning, do not get stuck on it. Keep a note book and keep writing the words you don't understand in it or simply underline the words on the text itself. Then go back later after reading the material once and find out the meaning of these terms. These are words whose meanings you should know so that the material makes sense to you so don't skip it either.

Do not try to pronounce each word–whether loudly or in your head: This habit of pronouncing each word internally in our head or loudly slows the process of reading. So do not indulge in it. Rather, just let your eyes glide on the sentences block by block and you will find yourself reading faster and with greater concentration.

Avoid the tendency to skip back: Most of us are lured towards re-reading or skipping back to previous lines. To reduce the number of times that your eyes skip back to a previous sentence, run a pointer along the line as you read. This could be a finger, or a pen or pencil. Your eyes will follow the tip of your pointer, smoothing the flow of your reading. The speed at which you read using this method will largely depend on the speed at which your hand guides the pointer.

The idea is to read fast but also to gather enough relevant information from the text. So master the trick of reading fast and you will find yourself with so much more extra time and yet ready for those exams.

❑❑❑

28

ANALYZE STUDY MATERIAL

In today's world a number of schools encourage or have already implemented various research programmes during the course of academics. While completing your project, you may feel the need to refer a senior's journal and see how it was designed? Whether you make use of a journal or any other kind of research material, read the following tips on how to analyze research study materials effectively.

Overview the structure of a research study material: Normally, research study material or a journal will consistently contain the following sections: Abstract, Introduction, Methods, Results, Discussion, and References. Some section names may change slightly, *e.g.* Methods might be Research Methods or Methodology.

ABSTRACT

Summary of the key points of the article: the purpose of the study and a hypothesis, the methodology used, what was studied, and the findings. Read this first, but don't rely on it solely to draw conclusions about the study.

INTRODUCTION

Normally, the introductory part of a research material contains a survey of relevant background for a study, a context for the study, and the hypothesis (*i.e.* the specific predictions to be tested). It will also usually contain a review of prior studies related to the same topic.

METHODS

It describes the approach to be taken in the study. This section provides detailed information about the research instrument used, (*e.g.* questionnaire), subjects (*e.g.* men between the ages of 20 and 40), procedures, and the approach to data analysis.

RESULTS

Data is summarized in this section, and relationships among variables and/or differences among groups are reported. This analysis should directly reflect the predictions originally described in the Introduction. Further comparisons may also be included to clarify findings or to explore unanticipated findings.

REFERENCES

It contains listing of the sources cited in the article such as books and articles, as well as sources not directly used but something which is relevant to the topic.

Note: Use the Reference list to find still other sources on your topic.

While reading

- Get as familiar as you can with the subject. Start with the Abstract for an overview.
- Read the first paragraph of the Introduction to get a sense of the issue. Go to the last paragraph to read the hypothesis.
- Skim the Discussion to see how the study turned out.
- Now, go back to the middle part for the details. Read the Methods section carefully and plan to re-read it, even a couple of times to digest it all.
- Start reading the Results section. You may want to turn to the Discussion section for clarification of what the reported statistics demonstrate. Don't get irritated by either the Methods or the Results section, but try to get a good idea of how the hypotheses were tested.
- Read the Discussion section more closely.
- Finally, read the whole article, first page to last page. Re-read for the greatest comprehension.

❑❑❑

29

BEST WAY TO LEARN

When asked to comment on the importance of critical thinking, the Chinese thinker and philosopher Confucius, known for his wise ways, replied, "It is like (learning without critical thinking) learning without thought, which means labour is lost."

- Critical thinking has assumed greater importance in today's day and time when one must consciously and deliberately apply reason and logic to what is being taught.
- Learning simply for the sake of it defeats the purpose of knowledge.
- Knowledge must find practical application otherwise it is reduced to cumbersome deadwood.
- Critical thinking is that cutting edge tool which helps choose between learning by rote and gleaning knowledge. When applied consciously and constructively, critical thinking beats out the chaff, leaving behind pure grains of wisdom.
- According to a popular and accepted description, 'critical thinking is the deliberate determination of whether we should accept, reject, or suspend judgment about a claim, and the degree of confidence with which we accept or reject it.'

After reading a subject, practice understanding it from the following perspectives:

- What is the issue?
- What are the official conclusions?
- What are the author's reasons for believing in certain theories?
- Do not follow the author's dictums blindly. Keep a lookout for bad reasoning that may mislead you from the central issue. It is a mistake to just pick up some reading material and just start reading. This method is not only time consuming

since it takes up a lot of time till the individual gets attuned to the subject matter, but less rewarding too. As a better alternative, it would be best to take off a minute or two to overview the text. Read and absorb the title, headings and summary to better understand the gist of the text. This way you will effortlessly glide into the theme as the author paints it and will be able to absorb ideas proposed in a better manner. This will also be helpful when one has been putting off text that one finds impossible to follow and comprehend. The overview is almost akin to tasting a food preparation before eating it; your 'taste buds' wake up to the senses and you want more.

CHECK YOUR COMPREHENSION

Before going from one major topic to the next, stop and analyze your comprehension of the subject.

- Ask yourself a few basic questions framed from major headings in the text.
- If you have a fair picture of the answer in your mind, be rest assured, you have really 'read' the text and are now ready to proceed further.
- If on the other hand you find you are not able to answer the questions satisfactorily, go back, do a once over and try to do better this time.

This can be done with story books as well as study material. Even though we do enjoy reading stories we are not able to recall details after some time. This technique will ensure that such a lapse doesn't occur. If you are part of a group that is reading /studying the same material together you could device a game of asking each other the questions.

REMEMBER WHAT YOU READ

Before embarking on reading anything get into the habit of asking yourself a question. Ask yourself why is it that you are reading?

This method of establishing the purpose of reading gives the mind a focus as how to read and what to look for while reading.

You will surprise yourself with the different kinds of information that you can glean from the same reading material when you pursue the reading with different purposes in mind. For example, if you are going through the dictionary to look up a particular word you will be reading very fast and will be disregarding unnecessary information as soon as it catches your eye.

But if you are reading the same dictionary to find an unusual word from say 'z' you will be looking more specifically. And once you start reading with this focus in mind you will find yourself more efficient.

Avoid reading unnecessary material, this distorts you focus and misleads you.

❑❑❑

30

GUARANTEE TO SUCCESS

Are you always postponing assignments and lessons for a later date? So what happens to your desk and time? The desk ends up looking like Mount Everest with the pile of pending work and time seems to be always flowing out thick and fast...beyond your control! Well, there is a cure to this problem. The remedy is – self discipline. And contrary to popular belief it is not difficult to inculcate self-discipline. It is just a matter of implementing it in small doses, regularly and persistently. You may undoubtedly have envied others for the amount of self-discipline they possess. No one is born with self discipline it has to be cultivated over the years. Those who seem to have mastered the art of self-discipline simply have more practice at it. Practice after all does make one perfect!

When you hate getting started on a task

- If you find yourself disinclined to do something important that needs to be done.
- Take a few minutes to talk to yourself rationally.
- Honestly pinpoint the real reason and the excuse as to why you are putting off the study.
- Once you are able to sift reason from excuse, you will find it relatively easier to tackle the reason and then go ahead and get your study done.

For example, you might be putting off going to the library telling yourself that you are too tired, but deep inside you are a bit terrified whether you will be able to find the right book in the right way. Once you acknowledge this you might take a friend along or ask for directions boldly and get your job done.

Don't expect too much of yourself. You will certainly find it hard to focus on studies from the very first day, and forcing yourself to do so will only make it harder to overcome the shift in lifestyle. Give yourself time to ease into the process and it should be easier for you.

After a while, your teachers and parents will surely expect you to start getting serious about exams and studies. You will need to do this, so do start the process early. Instead of waiting until the week before exams to study, and letting the transition drag on, start getting serious about school work after the first two weeks or so. Begin with becoming regular with your homework. Once you get used to doing a little work everyday, start studying for your exams. Remember, exams always come sooner than you think!

Finally, at some point, leave yourself no choices. Simply do not indulge yourself and let yourself laze around or daydream about your vacations when in class. Force yourself to cut down on recreation time and focus on work, so that you aren't under excessive pressure when exams come around.

Planning and a little self discipline will help you to be a Grade 'A' student!

❑❑❑

31

MAINTAIN YOUR NOTEBOOKS

The maintenance of your notebooks and presentation of your notes play as important a role as their contents in impressing instructors. Teachers often have to check a number of notebooks every day, and so standing out through presentation becomes extremely important. Here are few tips that are sure to help you master the much-desired art of impeccable maintenance and presentation:

Cover your notebooks with brown paper and plastic sheets: Notebooks are an invaluable record of successful strategies and reflective summaries. Hence, it becomes important to preserve them. Cover them to maintain in a premium state. If you can laminate your notebooks then nothing like it. Laminating over the brown paper helps in making the notebooks waterproof.

Always keep your notes complete: If you miss a class, ensure that you take notes from a batch mate at the earliest. Maintaining continuity of your notes is essential. Incomplete notes will bother you when you study for the exams and will also irritate your instructor.

Use a good pen: A ballpoint pen or a thin, smooth nib fountain or a pilot pen is preferable. A good pen ensures that your writing is uniform, continuous and flawless. Be careful not to let the ink blot in case of fountain pens.

Avoid scribbling and over-writing: Scribbling, cutting and then writing and over writing– all these make notebooks look untidy and unimpressive. The first rule for impressive and well-maintained notebooks is to be extremely careful while writing so that you don't have to scribble, cut and overwrite. If you have by chance written something wrong and you have to scratch it out, just strike the unwanted words with a single stroke and move on.

Underline and highlight essential matter: No teacher/instructor has the time to read through your entire mass of notes these days. If you underline the important points and highlight the summary, they are bound to take notice and get impressed. Also, this format is helpful during exams as it accelerates revision. Ensure that these underlined points are apt and correct and that the highlighted matter is well written.

A well-maintained notebook is a key to success so you should treat its maintenance as your priority. This will be your first step to academic success.

❑❑❑

32

MAKE MAXIMUM FROM LECTURES

Lecturers do not always deal with their ideas in a logical and consistent way. However, lectures are always informative and with the help of the following tips on note making and editing, you can definitely help yourself and others to make the best use of a lecture.

Before the lecture: Use a large, loose-leaf notebook. Use only one side of the paper. (You then can lay your notes out to see the direction of a lecture.) Draw a vertical line 2 1/2 inches from the left side of your paper. This is the recall column. Notes will be taken to the right of this margin. Later key words or phrases can be written in the recall column.

During the lecture: Record notes in paragraph form. Capture general ideas, not illustrative ideas. Skip lines to show end of ideas or thoughts. Using abbreviations will save time. Write legibly.

After the lecture: Immediately after the lecture you can recall which parts of the lecture were unclear to you so that you can consult the lecturer, a classmate, your text, or additional readings for further information. For better retention, review your notes immediately. Unless a student reviews within 24 hours after the lecture or at least before the next lecture, his retention is likely to drop; and he will be relearning rather than reviewing.

Editing notes: A method of annotation is highly preferred to recopy your notes. Make a habit of underlining key statements or important concepts. Always use asterisks or other signal marks to indicate importance. Use margins or blank pages for organizing notes with the text. Perhaps indicate relevant pages of the text beside the corresponding information in the notes. If necessary, use a key and a summary.

Making the final copy: Use one margin to keep a key of important names, formulas, dates and concepts. This enables you to look forward to questions of an objective nature and provides specific facts that you need to develop essays. Employ the other margin to write a short summary of the topics on the page, relating the contents of the page to the entire lecture or to the lecture of the day before. Condensing the notes in this way not only helps you to learn them but also prepares you for the kind of thinking required to succeed in subjective and objective exams.

❑❑❑

33

ENJOY YOUR PROGRESS

As you progress through your work take that occasional look over your shoulder and give yourself a pat on the back for whatever you have achieved. As a result you will approach the remainder of the task with considerably more enthusiasm. This will hold true for both small and large tasks performed. The pat on the back will give you a boost of self-confidence, increase your feeling of self worth and as a result you will be ready to take on more. Self-appreciation is the most truthful form of appreciation and you know it. So when you are able to appreciate yourself it means you have really done something worthwhile.

WILL POWER AND PATIENCE

There is no replacement of strong will, determination and a vision of success to succeed. The attitude is not required merely when it comes to studies but in life in general. One must work consistently to a goal to achieve it, you cannot have pipe dreams of success and expect to attain it. Success is moulded in the mind and takes concrete form as achievement later. Besides a will to succeed what is also essential is the endurance and patience to bear with failure. The best example of determination and patience that one can possibly cite is that of King Bruce, who after having lost virtually everything in war was inspired to regain his lost wealth by a spider.

ANALYSE YOUR MOTIVATION

When you are about to start a new assignment, just stop and spare a few minutes for the thought "Why am I doing this–because I want to or because I have to?" Past experience will tell you that whenever you have done something that you really want to it has been done well, however difficult the task may have been. And if something was done just because it needed to be done the enthusiasm accompanying the performance would be missing and the performance would leave a lot to be desired. So when faced with such a task that needs to be done despite how you feel about it, analyse why it needs to be done. The logic will add lustre to the task and eventually you will want to do it.

HOLISTIC LEARNING

Education is all about creating and nurturing a positive and focused attitude that helps in the holistic development of a person rather than a particular faculty only. Here are a few ways to make your education process a holistic exercise:

Besides gleaning knowledge on a subject, it is essential to cultivate qualities like positive attitude, discipline, quality and self gratification (that follows a well done job).

Having a flexible attitude and adaptability to go a long way. It must be cultivated by students at an early stage.

Demonstrating a desire to learn is essential to gleaning holistic knowledge. Do not, for example take the easier path of guides and old question papers. Understand thoroughly and then use the question papers as a tool for brushing up.

Being a team worker is another important attitude which a student must develop.

Being a part of larger social activities like projects, social gatherings, school festivals are ways to develop interpersonal relations. Students must take pro-active steps to be a part of these.

TIP TOP, NEAT AND CLEAN

Being prim and proper gives you an added advantage over your peers. Everybody likes dealing with those who maintain themselves. Clean and cut your nails, polish your shoes, wear a clean uniform, in short be clean so that you feel fresh. The attitude will reflect even in the way you treat your books and is sure to win you laurels.

DON'T STAMMER

First and foremost try to look beyond the stammering. Concentrating too hard on this setback only aggravates the problem, which becomes even more pressing during oral exams. Relax, and try to think of the correct answer to the question (during exams) rather than concentrating on the stammering problem. In case the problem persists, smile–it works wonders.

DON'T PLAY TRUANT

Be alert and active and don't skip class. Being regular and punctual has its own benefits that will help to gain that extra edge over your classmates. Being alert also means that you don't have to stay up late hours in the night to mug up lessons, which you could have understood, by simply staying alert in class. Not playing truant also has its other merits, escaping the cane just happens to be the most important amongst them.

❑❑❑

34

USE INTERNET WISELY

Finding information on the Internet is fairly easy, as long as you realize what you are searching and can judge what you find. Remember that the Internet is not an edited, ordered, or unified information package like a set of encyclopedias. The Internet supports a wide range of human communication, and this communication reflects all the foibles, intelligence, stupidity, wisdom, aggressiveness, kindness, malevolence, and chaos of human life.

You can think of the Internet more as a vibrant city than as an ordered set of books. As you go to city in your daily life, you don't believe everything you hear, read, or see. You are wary of strangers and seek out trusted places to do business, shop, or make friends. Have this same kind of sensibility on the Internet.

You can follow these ideas to improve your information literacy in using Internet information:

- What is the source of information? What are the sources of qualifications, motivations, and likely biases? Be sophisticated and wary about what information sources you consult. Start with trusted information sources. For example, large public libraries have Web sites that might be good starting point to locate information.
- What degree of reliability and accuracy do you need for your information? Do you need information from an expert in the field? Or are you just looking for ideas? For example, if you are getting ideas for your garden, you might want to consult an expert for information on chemicals and fertilizers. In this case, try the Web sites of major gardening magazines. If you want ideas about what flowers to plant, you might find a fellow gardener's site serves your needs perfectly.

- What is the quality and value of information? If you are satisfied with the reputation of the source, what can you do with the information? Is the information current, accurate, and well-organized so that it is useful to you? All of this will depend on the information. Current temperatures in your city? That information has to be very recent (like within the past hour) for it to be useful to you. Ideas for new kinds of mulch? A Web page that is a year or two old might be just fine.

Have you checked out other information sources? Use multiple strategies to find information and compare information from multiple sites. You may find reputable and knowledgeable sites like libraries or specialized magazines recommend certain sites repeatedly. You can compare suggestions from several sites to make your final decision. In a way, you have to be like a good journalist on the Internet: locate several reliable sources.

You should have some sites in mind to help you search the Internet subject, keyword, and reference information.

Once you are comfortable with using the Internet for e-mail and the Web for information, you can establish routines that benefit your life. You can search the Web regularly for news, shopping, employment, education, or your hobby needs. If you have an e-mail address, be sure to check your account a couple of times per week for incoming mail.

But be wary of excessive use—don't let the Internet take over your life. Don't use the Web as a kind of mindless stimulation like television. Check your e-mail or find what you need on the Web. Then get out and do something in the real world.

TIPS

- Use a reputed browser *e.g.* Internet Explorer version 6.0.
- Use the latest version that supports secure transactions.
- Update the browser with the latest patch from the respective authorized browser sites.
- Install a reputed licensed anti-virus software and regularly update it with the latest definitions.
- Do not ever click on a link that you get through e-mail especially for shopping or financial sites; go the concerned site by typing the correct address on to the web browser and access that site.
- Install reputed personal firewalls especially when you use broadband connection; (Broadband connection—the connection to the internet is always on *e.g.* through cable or leased line unlike dialup where you connect to the internet by connecting through normal telephone lines.
- Firewall in brief is usually a software used that can specify which are the sites that are allowed to be accessed or denied; this will help in further protecting your computer.
- Do not use public PCs to access important internet sites or conduct online shopping.
- Do not give your password or pin to any person.
- Do not randomly allow any person to access your computer.
- Do not install any kind of unlicensed or pirated software.
- Do not open e-mail or its attachment from any unknown person; be careful with attachments even from known person.
- If you use broadband connection do not share your computer or keep the connection live when you do not need internet.
- Do your shopping only from reputed merchants.
- When you do your online shopping always ensure that the website begins with https and not http.
- Check the website of merchants to ensure that the certificate is current before doing shopping.

- Make your payment only through reputed financial institutions.
- Always logout after using online e-mail or shopping or financial transaction.
- Always use highest security option when you use online e-mail.
- Always choose password or username that are not easily available *e.g.* you must not use your date of birth, spouse name, telephone number or city of birth.
- Do check the degree of online security used by the financial institution *e.g.* does it use 128 bit SSL.
- Immediately inform your bank about change in your address or e-mail ID.
- Go through terms of use of any site specially those that you use regularly.
- Do not share your computer with any other person and if you do want to share, please ensure that such sharing is password protected.
- Do not reply to, or click on links within, e-mails or pop-up messages that ask for sensitive information such as passwords, debit card numbers, credit card numbers etc.
- Do regularly update your browsers such as Internet Explorer or Mozilla Firefox with authorised patches directly from respective websites.
- Do shred, or otherwise destroy, all documents with personal information prior to disposal.
- Do monitor your bank account and credit card statements/ account at frequent intervals and if any incorrect transaction is recorded the same to be checked with the concerned organisation immediately.
- Do not e-mail sensitive information such as your credit card number, debit card number, passwords, etc.
- Always keep a separate record of contact numbers as well as details of your sensitive information such as debit/credit card numbers so that you can immediately report loss of cards or misuse of cards.

❑❑❑

35

GOOD PRESENTATION OF THE ASSIGNMENT

To fail to prepare is to prepare to fail.

Great presentations require some preplanning. First, read meetings for an outline of preparing and conducting a meeting, such as acquiring a room, informing participants, etc. A presentation follows the same basic guidelines as preparing for a meeting.

The second step is to prepare the presentation. A good presentation starts out with introductions and an icebreaker such as a story, interesting statement or fact, joke, quotation, or an activity to get the group warmed up. The introduction also needs an objective, that is, the purpose or goal of the presentation. This not only tells you what you will talk about, but it also informs the audience of the purpose of the presentation.

Next comes the body of the presentation. Do not write it out word for word. All you want is an outline. By jotting down the main points on a set of index cards, you not only have your outline, but also a memory jogger for the actual presentation. To prepare the presentation, ask yourself the following:

- What is the purpose of the presentation?
- Who will be attending?
- What does the audience already know about the subject?
- What is the audience's attitude towards me (*e.g.* hostile, friendly)?

A 45 minutes talk should have no more than about seven main points. This may not seem like many, but if you are to leave the audience with a clear picture of what you have said, you cannot expect them to remember much more than that. There are several options for structuring the presentation:

Timeline: Arranged in sequential order.

Climax: The main points are delivered in order of increasing importance.

Problem/Solution: A problem is presented, a solution is suggested, and benefits are then given.

Classification: The important items are the major points.

Simple to complex: Ideas are listed from the simplest to the most complex. Can also be done in reverse order.

You want to include some visual information that will help the audience understand your presentation. Develop charts, graphs, slides, handouts, etc.

After the body, comes the closing. This is where you ask for questions, provide a wrap-up (summary), and thank the participants for attending.

Notice that you told them what they are about to hear (the objective), told them (the body), and told them what they heard (the wrap up).

And finally, the important part: practice, practice, practice. The main purpose of creating an outline is to develop a coherent plan of what you want to talk about. You should know your presentation so well, that during the actual presentation, you should only have to briefly glance at your notes to ensure that you are staying on track. This will also help you with your nerves by giving you the confidence that you can do it. Your practice session should include a 'live' session by practicing in front of classmates, family, or friends. They can be valuable at providing feedback and it gives you a chance to practice controlling your nerves. Another great feedback technique is to make a video or audio tape of your presentation and review it critically with a colleague.

TIPS

- If you have handouts, do not read straight from them. The audience does not know if they should read along with you or listen you to read.
- Do not put both hands in your pockets for long periods of time. This tends to make you look unprofessional. It is OK to put one hand in a pocket but ensure that there is no loose change or keys to jingle around. This will distract the listeners.
- Do not wave a pointer around in the air like a wild knight branding a sword to slay a dragon. Use the pointer for what it is intended and then put it down, otherwise the audience will become fixated upon your 'sword', instead upon you.
- Do not lean on the podium for long periods. The audience will begin to wonder when you are going to fall over.
- Speak to the audience...not to the visual aids, such as flip charts or overheads. Also, do not stand between the visual aid and the audience.
- Speak clearly and loudly enough for all to hear. Do not speak in a monotone voice. Use inflection to emphasize your main points.
- The disadvantages of presentation are that people cannot see the punctuation and this can lead to misunderstandings. An effective way of overcoming this problem is to pause at the time when there would normally be punctuation marks.
- Learn the name of each participant as quickly as possible. Based upon the atmosphere you want to create, call them by their first names or by using Mr., Mrs., Miss, Ms.
- Tell them what name and title you prefer to be called.
- Listen intently to comments and opinions. By using a *lateral thinking technique* (adding to ideas rather than dismissing them), the audience will feel that their ideas, comments, and opinions are worthwhile.

- Circulate around the room as you speak. This movement creates a physical closeness to the audience.
- List and discuss your objectives at the beginning of the presentation. Let the audience know how your presentation fits in with their goals. Discuss some of the fears and apprehensions that both you and the audience might have. Tell them what they should expect of you and how you will contribute to their goals.
- Vary your techniques (lecture, discussion, debate, films, slides, reading, etc.)
- Get to the presentation before your audience arrives; be the last one to leave.
- Be prepared to use an alternate approach if the one you've chosen seems to bog down. You should be confident enough with your own material so that the audience's interests and concerns, not the presentation outline, determines the format. Use your background, experience, and knowledge to interrelate your subject matter.
- When writing on flip charts use no more than 7 lines of text per page and no more than 7 words per line. Also, use bright and bold colours, and pictures as well as text.
- Consider the time of day and how long you have got for your talk. Time of day can affect the audience. After lunch is known as the graveyard section in training circles as audience will feel more like a nap than listening to a talk.

Most people find that if they practice in their head, the actual talk will take about 25 per cent longer. Using a flip chart or other visual aids also adds to the time. Remember—it is better to finish slightly early than to overrun.

❑❑❑

36

DEVELOP LEADERSHIP SKILLS

All cultures need role models and leaders. Most of us agree that professions such as medicine, technology, education, business and industry, politics, and the arts need people who can use intelligence, creativity, and critical judgment. The role of parents and educators is critical in assisting with the development of leadership attitudes and skills in gifted youth.

CHARACTERISTICS OF LEADERSHIP IN GIFTED YOUTH

Many characteristics of gifted youth enable them to profit from leadership development. Those characteristics include the following:

- The desire to be challenged.
- The ability to solve problems creatively.
- The ability to reason critically.
- The ability to see new relationships.
- Facility of verbal expression.
- Flexibility in thought and action.
- The ability to tolerate ambiguity.
- The ability to motivate others.

LEADERSHIP THROUGH EXTRA CURRICULAR ACTIVITIES

Since leadership is learned over time through involvement with others, extracurricular activities provide fertile ground for nurturing future leaders. Group participation offers unique opportunities for young people to belong, support others, and learn a variety of leadership styles. Students learn how to encourage others, create group spirit, and resolve conflict. They begin to understand diverse attitudes, skills, and talents and how to interact effectively with a diversity of people while working toward a common goal.

Leadership in extracurricular activities has been found to be more highly correlated with adult leadership than with academic achievement.

There are many organized extracurricular activities for youth, those who want to develop their leadership potential can do so through less formal methods. Individuals or groups can plan special projects or a leadership plan by setting goals, objectives, and timelines toward a mission of improving some area of the school or community. Skills such as seeking all available information, defining a group task, and devising a workable plan may be developed through any community project. No matter how small or large the goal, the process involved in devising and implementing the plan develops leadership potential.

Leadership is much more than being elected or appointed to a position and it is acquired most effectively through practice. Educators, parents, and other concerned adults who are interested in the development of leadership in gifted youth can make a difference in the lives of these students by providing them with opportunities to realize their leadership potential.

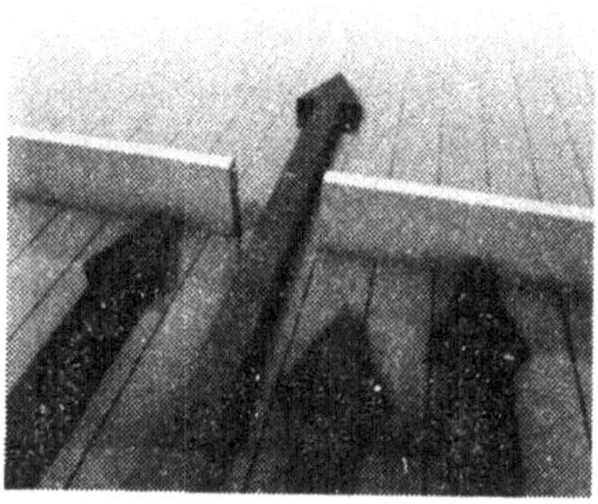

INFUSING LEADERSHIP CONCEPTS AND SKILLS INTO THE CURRICULUM

Major emphasis should be placed on leadership development in all academic areas, including the fine and performing arts. Thematic curriculum units and reading lists should include biographies and autobiographies of outstanding leaders. Students should be encouraged to analyze and evaluate the motivation, contributions, and influences of each leader and assess the leadership styles employed. Major events, family and other influences important in the life of each leader should be emphasized.

Sciences : Physical and biological sciences, mathematics, and social sciences provide unique opportunities for projects in which initiating, planning, critical thinking, creative problem solving, and decision making can be developed. They are rich with opportunities to learn about leaders who have influenced such areas as government and politics, science and technology, humanities and the arts, business and industry, philosophy and religion, and health science and medicine. Students can learn how their interests, passions, and abilities can develop into careers. They can compare the contributions of others with their own value systems. For example, many leaders have been concerned about poverty and the human condition.

Humanities: Language, arts, speech, English, and other courses that emphasize oral and written communication provide opportunities for potential leaders to learn how to present ideas clearly and persuasively. Preparing and presenting speeches, listening to and critiquing presentations, writing news reports and editorials for school and other local publications, preparing for and engaging in debates, leading conference and discussion sessions, and participating in school and other election campaigns are only a few of the many options available. Group activities provide opportunities for young people to learn how to help others, feel important and valued, accept their contributions, keep discussions relevant, and occasionally follow rather than lead.

Arts: Students can learn leadership skills and gain inspiration from talented people of the past and present who have enriched all of us through their contributions in the fine and performing arts. Their creative works, the trends they initiated, and the enduring results of their efforts are worthy of study, as are their lives and the circumstances under which their work came to fruition.

PARENTS AND THE DEVELOPMENT OF LEADERSHIP

Preparing young people for leadership responsibility begins in the home with an enriched environment that offers opportunities for children to acquire broad interests, self-esteem, and the insights and skills that characterize leaders. Parents can provide their children with support and encouragement as they participate in a wide variety of home and community activities. Parents should encourage their children to be involved in the selection, planning, execution, and evaluation of family activities ranging from a day at the zoo to a vacation overseas. Youngsters should also be encouraged to plan, initiate, and complete a variety of self-evaluated individual projects, but these skills are not learned automatically. They must be patiently taught and modeled by parents in the home.

Discussion and debate about current events and other topics foster independent thinking and nurture leadership potential. Parents, who listen openly and thoughtfully without expecting children to embrace their social, political, and economic views are demonstrating leadership characteristics. Mutual respect, objectivity, empathy, and understanding are highly valued by gifted young people, particularly those who need a safe place to test their ideas.

Opportunities for decision making at an early age will help to foster the critical reasoning skills necessary to be an effective leader. Inappropriate decisions by children and youth, although difficult for parents to accept, may enhance future decision-making skills when self-evaluated.

❑❑❑

37

AVOID SPELLING MISTAKES

Spelling errors are very distracting, whether you are reading or writing. Fair or not, people form impressions about your knowledge and intelligence based upon spelling. Here are some common spelling errors to avoid and tips on preventing future mistakes.

WHEN IN DOUBT, LEAVE APOSTROPHE OUT

The omitted apostrophe confuses meaning less often than the needless one does. If I write a note to tell you, "This is Ranjan's dog," you'll likely to know I mean to let you know the dog belongs to Ranjan. If I write instead, "Robert's friend's are writer's," and you know anything about the punctuation of English, you will be in some confusion as to what belongs to whom.

In general, the apostrophe means one of two things.

1. There is a missing letter where it is. For example, in 'don't' there is a missing 'o'; in 'it's' there is a missing 'I': each of these is a one-word contraction commonly used to represent two words. 'Don't' means 'do not', and 'it's' means 'it is'.

2. Something belongs to someone. For example, 'Ranjan's dog' means the dog belongs to Ranjan. 'Karim's house' means the house belongs to Karim (or at least that he lives in it). Apostrophe-S is used to indicate *possession.*

Number 2 above presents a problem when a thing belongs to a thing. If we want to say, 'The box has its label now', shouldn't we use 'it's' to show possession? The answer is most emphatically no, we should not. 'It's' means 'it is'. It *never* means 'belonging to it'.

And here I present you with a secret about apostrophes: if the reader sees none where there should be one, he/she will imagine you've dropped it by accident, and that the result is a typographical error rather than an indication of ignorance.

But if he/she sees an apostrophe where there should be none, she is unlikely to imagine that you added it by accident. Even if in this one case you really *did* hit that key without noticing, your reader is going to assume that you did it deliberately, in ignorance. It is a sad truth about readers. As a result, you're much safer if you follow the apostrophe rule: *when in doubt, leave it out.*

- Know when to use 'to.' This is one of the most common spelling mistakes. You should use "too" when you are talking about something in excess, or to mean 'also'. For example, you might write, 'The chocolate is too hard', or 'I like candies too.' The appropriate way to use 'to' is when something is going to something else. You could write, 'I gave my card collection to Bobby', or 'I am going to the mall'.
- Avoid the extra letter O. Use 'lose' when referring to something that has been lost. 'Loose' applies when something is not as tight as it should be.
- Be careful to use an apostrophe when you need one. Many people confuse 'your' and 'you're'. An apostrophe should be used when two words are joined together and one or more letters are removed. 'You're' is short for 'you are', so it needs an apostrophe. If you wrote 'I gave it to your mother' you would not use an apostrophe. The same rule applies for 'their' and 'they're'.
- Get someone to read/edit your writing if you are in doubt about your spelling. Someone who is looking over your writing with a fresh pair of eyes can see things that you missed, even though you read over it several times.
- Keep a dictionary handy, and when in doubt, check the word for accurate spelling.
- If working on a computer use your word processor's spell check function. This prevents many spelling mistakes.

TOP 11 SPELLING ERRORS

Is there anything worse than leaving a careless spelling or grammatical error in your writings? You may proof the page ten times without finding it, but your teacher will find it immediately and be angry with you.

Here are the top ten errors you're likely to notice when visiting web pages or going through an article or checking your classmates writing assignment. Use it as a beginning checklist to eliminate spelling and grammar errors from your own writings.

1. It's and Its

This is such a common error that you should routinely use the search function on your word processor or Web page editor to look at every instance individually to make sure you're using the correct word.

It's is a contraction meaning "it is" while *its* is the possessive form of *it*.

It's never a good idea to get between a dog and its favourite chew.

2. You, Your, and You're

This is another very common error that needs to be checked using the search function. While the previous example is a grammatical error, the confusion of *you* and *your* is usually a typographical error. *You're* is the contraction of "you are" and some people confuse it with *your*.

Since all three words are spelled correctly, spell checkers won't flag them. Then you end up with jewels like this on your Web page:

Don't delay! Place you order now! We offer free home delivery if your in India.

Would you trust your credit card to that site?

3. Lose and Loose

- *Loose* can have several meanings in English and is used as an adjective, adverb, or a verb (although that's not very common). *Unattended children ran loose through the toy store.*
- *She hated the street seller and regularly loosed her dogs on him.*
- *That group of teens has a pretty loose reputation.*

But *lose* is always a verb:

- *His mother told him to lose the attitude or else.*
- *The team never believed that they'd lose the game.*
- *I was so happy to lose the extra 20 pounds I'd been carrying since my stay abroad.*

4. Compliment and Complement

These two homophones trip up even the most careful writers.

If you like your brother's new drawing, you'll compliment him on his art skills.

Complement has meanings in grammar, medicine, mathematics, and music, but it's most commonly used to indicate that something completes a set or matches it well.

When you compliment your brother's drawing, you might note how well the soft green colour complements the off-white.

5. Principal and Principle

A *principle* is a basic truth, policy, or action. People dedicate their lives and careers to upholding *principles* of truth and justice. *Principals* are people who uphold standards of good behaviour in schools.

A school's principal should always stick to her principles.

6. Except and Accept

Except connotes exclusion or something left out, like an exception to the rule.

Accept means that you're receiving something, joining a group, entering into an agreement, etc.

I'd accept your marriage proposal- except for one problem. I'm already married.

7. Affect and Effect

Affect is a verb: It acts upon something, someone, or an emotion, while *effect* is a noun. The words sound almost identical in conversation, but it's important to get them right in print!

The discovery that his wife could control the weather affected her husband rather badly.

The so-called 'Wealth Effect' affected total consumer spending and debt levels far more than economists anticipated.

8. Peak and Pique

A *peak* is the top of a mountain or the highest point in something's development or intensity. *Pique* refers to an emotion—usually anger or curiosity.

In a fit of pique, the rock climber hurled his partner's favourite harness off the highest peak.

9. Assure, Insure and Ensure

Assure, ensure, and insure all mean 'to make secure or certain'. Only *assure* is used with reference to a person in the sense of 'to set the mind at rest': *assured the leader of his loyalty.* Although *ensure* and *insure* are generally interchangeable, only *insure* is now widely used in American English in the commercial sense of 'to guarantee persons or property against risk'.

I assure you that the insured property owner is taking steps to ensure your safety.

10. Moot and Mute

How often have you heard someone insist: 'it's a *mute* point!' Well, if it's a topic that's incapable of making a sound, they're correct. But more often they're really trying to say that it's a *moot* point—or one that's irrelevant.

Since the point was already moot, Raman stood mutely in front of the teacher.

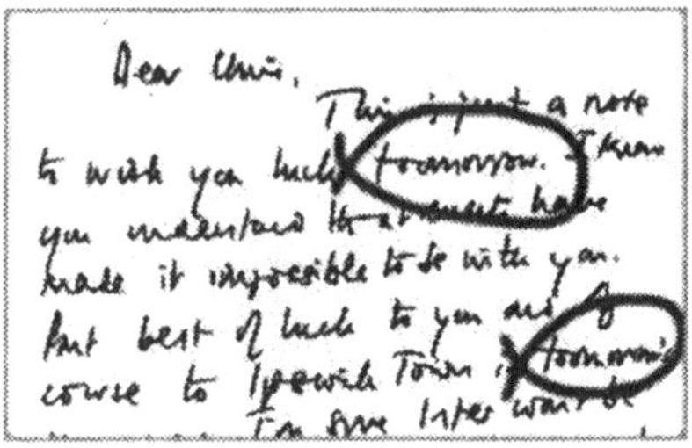

11. Me, Myself and I

You see a lot of usage errors with these three words. Generations of school children grew used to constant correction about the use of *me* in sentences. While most learned that *'Sandy and me want to go'* is incorrect, they never learned the correct usage of the word *me*.

Would you please call Sandy or me before you leave? is perfectly clear and acceptable.

Yet, well-meaning people substitute either *I* or the reflexive pronoun *myself* instead. How often do you hear or read something like this:

Would you please call Sandy or myself before you leave?

Take Sandy out of the sentence and you're either asking the person to *'call I before you leave'* or *call myself before you leave'*. Neither one sounds or looks very attractive.

Don't be afraid to use the word *me* in sentences, but take care to use it correctly!

In the last you must remember—Unfortunately, even the best spell checker won't find these errors.

38

MAINTAIN BALANCE IN STUDY & SPORTS

Many students play sports and go to school at the same time. This is fun, but often we find that the balance scale is tipped towards sports instead of school. Academics should always be first in life, no matter what the circumstances.

You can't shortchange school for athletics. Sometimes you may even have to give up a sport to regain what you have lost in the learning process when assignments don't get done or lessons aren't remembered. There are ways, however, to stop the problem before it begins. Here are a few of them.

1. Never spend too much time on sports: Many players practice all afternoon after school, every day, cutting into homework and study time. Instead of using all your time practicing, finish your homework, review the day's lessons, and take another look at tomorrow's assignments to make sure you've got everything covered. Many players put off homework until the last minute, when they arrive home, tired and hungry after hours of football or cricket practice. Postponing homework is the foundation for falling behind. Finish homework first before or after practice.

2. Always pay attention in class: Students who are involved in extra curricular activities often daydream about games or doze from being tired. There is a time for everything, so during school hours, remember to focus completely on school work. This will help because when doing your homework later, you'll understand it better than if you weren't paying attention in class. When at study hall, skim a lesson. When you have free time, take a few notes. You don't have to study all the time, but the more you do, the better off you'll be. You will play better knowing that your grades are going well, and your coach may be able to help get a tutor or suggest a mentor. Coaches love it when players are good students.

3. Know when to quit: This may seem harsh, but if you simply can't follow sports and studies, sports can be followed later. School has a long term scope, sports hasn't. It is well known that good-paying jobs are harder to find. You have to hone your skills before applying for a job. Take advantage of your universal education. If you do drop your sport, spend the former practice time catching up in your grades, then you can join the team next year, or play for a community league later. You have the rest of your life to play. Pursuing a school certificate gets harder as you get older. Get it while you can.

If you follow these steps and apply them when necessary, your grades should go up and you'll be happier. It is always better to have a good future than a great past. Your education should always go first no matter what the circumstances. It is also recommended talking to a teacher to discuss how to balance the two. School is cool! That is why you should choose to learn first.

❑❑❑

39

MAKE BEST OF YOUR SUMMER VACATIONS

It's hard to believe that the school year is weeks away from ending for another year! However, these days are the perfect time to think about how your student will spend their summer vacation. There are lots of opportunities available for kids these days, and the best choices are those things that help to keep their brains and bodies active and ready for the next school year! Before you sign your child up for endless weeks of arts and crafts, or become tired of watching them crash in front of the television all day long, consider these summer vacation ideas that can keep your child's mind healthy and active, too.

School Sponsored Day Camps

Many schools offer day programmes for students. Some schools offer academic programmes, ranging from remedial academic programmes to accelerated learning seminars. Other programmes focus on entertainment options that combine educational activities and fun. Depending on the needs of your child and the offerings of your school, consider allowing your child to participate this year. Most offerings are relatively inexpensive, many are staffed or run by certified teachers, and some offer extended hours of day care for parents, too.

Volunteering

Does your child have a passion for animals? Are they caring and sensitive to others? Are they creative and artistic? Consider finding out more about ways your child may be able to spare some of their summer vacation times and talents for social causes. Depending on your time availability and child's interests, there are many different volunteering options available for young people today.

Community Groups

Many community groups offer various programmes for students in the summer. Some community learning centres or small, local businesses may offer art classes or pottery classes. Other organizations such as Girl Scouts or Boy Scouts offer camp and leadership programmes for their members. Local YMCA groups usually offer a number of programmes for both boys and girls to enjoy. Some youth groups even continue to run activities and camps in the summer months to keep children happy, busy and safe during vacation. Check your local community groups to see if there is something right for your child.

Financial Note about Summer Programmes

Many parents do not even try to locate summer programmes in their area due to the expense they fear they cannot afford, yet summer programmes help to keep children's minds, social skills, and bodies healthy and active. Before rejecting the idea of summer programmes completely, find out if the sponsoring organization provides scholarships, payment plans, multiple child discounts or a sliding scale fee based on family income. Also, some programmes that run only mornings or afternoons or are only for a few days are considerably less expensive than those that run all day for the whole summer. Try to contact several different agencies or groups to determine if there is a local programme that can meet your child's needs without crushing your budget. Some local organizations may also be willing to sponsor your child. Don't give up a dream of summer fun before trying to contact these local agencies for help.

❑❑❑

40

COPING WITH SUMMER VACATION

School vacation doesn't mean a vacation from learning. As a matter of fact, it is impossible to stop a child from learning. That's what kids do. They learn from their parents, books, peers and play.

Nearly two months is a long time for children to go without any structured instruction. I see two kinds of kids by the end of the summer: One group is bored to the max. The others are so over-programmed they feel like they haven't had a vacation at all.

Strive for a happy medium. Give your children the opportunity to attend summer classes, day camps or sports instructions. But be sure they have plenty of time to learn and do things on their own.

Summer is the perfect time to encourage hobbies which kids do on their own like collecting bugs, or writing to pen pals, or studying dinosaurs. But it's also a good time to work along side their parents to learn some grownup stuff like cooking or carpentry.

Planning a family vacation? Let the kids map the route, calculate what gas will cost, and learn a bit about the locations to be visited.

Thinking about a big project you've been putting off forever like labeling old family photos or sorting recipes? Involve the kids. They can learn about Great Grandpa and his farm and realize you have to read and know how to measure in order to make a pie.

Even though it's summer remember the library is still open. A wise mother asks her children to read one book of their choice every week and writes a short report. This replaces those summer reading lists we got when I was a girl.

Summer is a good time to start a family book group. Each person reads aloud from a favorite book and then you talk about the book. Alternatively try a family story-telling time when each person tells a story. You can have themes like telling the scariest story or telling a story that takes place on another planet.

The idea is to see that all these activities are fun. And even when you are part of the fun let the children figure things out on their own rather than be taught.

Don't let such summer learning cut too deeply into do-nothing time. Don't let summer equal unlimited TV watching. TV rules are in effect all year long.

While summer vacation can be relaxing times for sleeping in, eating home-cooked meals, and seeing old friends; for many students it may fall significantly short of the romanticized image. Issues that students often face can be discussed under three different headings:

FAMILY AND HOME

When returning home from college, a period of readjustment is natural and expected. After a year away, you may have changed from the person your family remembers. Sometimes parents feel threatened by such changes, perhaps feeling a loss of control, fearing of your new independence, or feeling devalued in their parental role. Even the best families occasionally struggle with such tensions, which need not become insurmountable rifts. If talked about with mutual caring and respect, such tensions and changes can provide the basis for a more mature and equal relationship. In this way, your own development as a person may contribute to your parents' growth as they face the inevitable challenge of their own shifting roles.

WORK

Looking for a job—whether be it for the summer or a career following graduation—is a major rite of passage. This rite, which marks the passage into adulthood, challenges us to demonstrate who we are and what we know to the larger world. We are also challenged to maintain our self-esteem and sense of perspective in the face of evaluation and possible rejection. Although summer employment is less an indication of one's social status and success than launching one's career, it is easy to become caught up in the process finding the perfect summer job. One way to avoid the roller-coaster of expectation and disappointment is to keep in mind that every loss or closed door is also an opportunity. Obstacles teach us to become more resilient, flexible, and creative—qualities whose value will last far longer than the three summer months. Even unemployment can teach us such lessons as humility and valuing the moment, instilling in us a confidence in our ability to survive our worst fears. The next time one of your hopes or expectations is dashed against reality, you might ask yourself: what opportunities do this leave open? Perhaps, you will be surprised by what you discover.

SOCIAL LIFE AND RECREATION

It seems to defy common sense to suggest that many of us struggle more with having free time on our hands than with being intensely busy. And yet, the sudden lack of structure that accompanies extended vacations poses a real challenge for many people. Some students even experience depression, as personal issues that were submerged under the demands of school and work suddenly rise to the surface. Since most of us were raised in a system that tends to organize our time for us, many of us have not learned to structure our free time in ways that are personally gratifying. Leaving new friends behind and discovering that old friends have moved or changed, can also leave us facing a social vacuum. Again, while this loss may be frustrating and painful; it also presents opportunities, such as discovering new interests, stretching our social horizons, or letting ourselves explore the places and pursuits that live only in our fantasy life. And if you feel stuck, remember: who is holding you back, if not yourself?

❑❑❑

41

HOMEWORK AND STUDY HABITS

Certain key practices will make life easier for everyone in the family when it comes to study time and organization. However, some of them may require an adjustment for other members of the family.

Turn off the TV set. Make a house rule, depending on the location of the set, that when it is study time, it is 'no TV' time. A television set that is on will draw youngsters like bees to honey.

What about the radio? Should it be on or off? Contrary to what many specialists say, some youngsters do seem to function all right with the radio turned on to a favourite music station.

Certain rules should be set about the family phone during study hours. The more people in the household, the more restrictions on long and unnecessary phone calls are needed. A timer, placed next to the phone, can help to control the length of calls so that the telephone will be available if it becomes necessary to call a schoolmate to confirm an assignment or discuss particularly difficult homework.

Designate specific areas for homework and studying. Possibilities include the child's room or the kitchen or dining room table. Eliminate as much distraction as possible.

Since many young people will study in their own rooms, function becomes more important than beauty. Most desks for young people really don't have sufficient space to spread out materials. A table that allows for all necessary supplies such as pencils, pens, paper, books, and other essentials work extremely well.

Consider placing a bulletin board in your child's room. Your local hardware store sells wallboard that might not look too pretty and isn't framed, but a 4x3' section is inexpensive and perfect on which to post pertinent school items. You might want to paint or cover it with burlap to improve its appearance or let your child take on this project.

Encourage the use of a small book or pad for writing down assignments so that there is no confusion about when certain assignments must be turned in to the teacher.

Keeping general supplies on hand is important. Check with your child about his needs. In fact, make it his responsibility to be well supplied with paper, pencils, note pads, notebook paper, et cetera.

Regularity is a key factor in academic success. Try to organize the household so that supper is served at a standard time, and once the family discussions are over, it's time to crack the books. If the student doesn't have other commitments and gets home reasonably early from school, some homework can be done before supper.

Consider your child's developmental level when setting the amount of time for homework. While high school students can focus for over an hour, first-graders are unlikely to last more than 15 minutes on a single task. Allow your child to take breaks, perhaps as a reward for finishing a section of the work.

Organize study and homework projects. Get a large calendar, one that allows space for jotting down things in the daily boxes. Rip it apart so that you (and the child) can sequentially mount the school months for the current semester. For example, you can tear off September, October, November, December, and January and mount them from left to right across one wall. Have the child use a bold colour writing instrument to mark exam dates in one colour, reports that are coming due in a different colour, etc. This will serve as a reminder so that things aren't set aside until the last dangerous moment.

Teach your child that studying is more than just doing homework assignments. One of the most misunderstood aspects of schoolwork is the difference between studying and doing homework assignments. Encourage your child to do things like:

- Take notes as he's reading a chapter
- Learn to skim material
- Learn to study tables and charts
- Learn to summarize what he has read in his own words
- Learn to make his own flashcards for quick review of dates, formulas, spelling words, et cetera

Note-taking is a critical skill and should be developed. Many students don't know how to take notes in those classes that require them. Some feel they have to write down every word the teacher says. Others have wisely realized the value of an outline form of note-taking. Well prepared teachers present their material in a format that lends itself to outline form of note taking.

Should notes ever be rewritten? In some cases, they should be, particularly if a lot of material was covered, and the youngster had to write quickly but lacks speed and organization. Rewriting notes takes time, but it can be an excellent review of the subject matter. However, rewriting notes isn't worth the time unless they are used for review and recall of important information.

A home dictionary is essential, but if it is kept on a shelf to gather dust, it won't do anyone any good. Keep it in an accessible place and let your child see you refer to it from time to time. If the family dictionary is kept in the living room and the child studies in his room, get him an inexpensive dictionary for his exclusive use.

Good dictionary, encyclopedia and organizational skills depend on the ability to alphabetize. See if your child's teacher practices alphabetizing in class. Try alphabetizing spelling words, family members' names or a few favourite toys at home as a way of practicing.

Help your child to feel confident for tests. Taking tests can be a traumatic experience for some students. Explain to your child that burning the midnight oil (cramming) the night before a test is not productive. It is better to get a good night's sleep. Students also need reminding that when taking a test, they should thoroughly and carefully read the directions before they haphazardly start to mark their test papers. They should be advised to skip over questions for which they don't know the answers. They can always return to those if there's time. Good advice for any student before taking a test: take a deep breath, relax, and dive in. Always bring an extra pencil just in case.

During a homework session, watch for signs of frustration. No learning can take place and little can be accomplished if the child is angry or upset over an assignment that is too long or too difficult. At such times the parent may have to step in and simply halt the homework for that night, offering to write a note to the teacher explaining the situation and perhaps requesting a conference to discuss the quality and length of homework assignments.

Should parents help with homework? Yes, if it is clearly productive to do so, such as calling out spelling words or checking a math problem that won't prove. No-if it is something the child can clearly handle himself and learn from the process. And help and support should always be calmly and cheerfully given. Grudging help is worse than no help at all!

Read directions, or check over math problems after your child has completed the work. Remember to make positive comments—you don't want your child to associate homework with fights at home.

Model research skills by involving your child in planning a family trip. Help your child to locate your destination on a map or atlas. Use traditional encyclopedia or a CD-ROM to find information about the place you will visit; try the Internet or books in the library.

How best to handle report cards? To save shocks and upsets, gently discuss from time to time "How things are going at school-with your child? Something casual, such as "How did the math test go?" "How did you do on the history report?" "How's your science project coming along? Need any help?" are questions that aren't 'third degree' but indicate interest. Find out if it is a policy at your child's school to send out "warning notices" when work isn't going well. Generally, such notices require the parent's signature to verify that the parent has, indeed, been alerted. This is the time to contact the teacher of the course, along with your child, to learn what the difficulty may be. If such notices aren't sent, then grades on projects and reports and from tests may be the sole source of information short of what your child wishes to share. Be tuned in to statements such as "He's an awful teacher," "She goes too fast," etc. This may be the child's way of indicating frustration in understanding content or lack of study time with the subject. However, be cautious in contacting teachers without your child's approval or interest. It may disrupt good feelings between you and make you seem to be interfering and spying.

❑❑❑

42

SCHOOL AND TEACHER RELATIONSHIPS

Researches show that one of the most important factors that affect a child's performance in school is parental involvement. All too often, parents assume that just sending their children to school and looking at their report cards is enough. Not true! If you want to be involved, if you want to actively participate in the relationship between your child and school, there are some things you can do to make this relationship positive and productive.

KNOW YOUR CHILD'S SCHOOL BETTER

- First of all, don't just show up at the school; make an appointment to visit.
- After you've made an appointment, go to the school; look around, talk to people.
- As appropriate, call or write to your child's teachers.
- Talk to other parents about their experiences.
- Be sure to read the minutes of the school board.
- It may not always be convenient, but try to attend school functions such as fetes, open houses and PTA meetings.

HOW CAN PARENTS HELP IN HOMEWORK?

There are things you can do that will help your child to do assigned homework that result in learning, which, after all, is the reason for being in school.

Communicate with your child about school. This includes talking to him about his friends, activities, teachers, and assignments.

Show enthusiasm about school and homework.

Set realistic goals for your child, and then focus on one at a time.

Help your child to get organized. Break down assignments into smaller, more manageable parts. Set out needed items (clothes, homework, permission slips, etc.) the night before to avoid last-minute rushing around in the morning.

Provide a quiet study corner in your home complete with paper, markers, a ruler, pencils and a dictionary.

Never do your child's homework!

Check with your child's teacher about correcting homework.

Expect, and praise **genuine** progress and effort. An opinion: don't praise or otherwise reward your child for doing what you and he **know is expected**. This practice leads you down a slippery slope, often with really bad consequences for you and your child.

Be specific when you do praise something.

Focus on your child's strengths in school.

Build associations between what is taught and what your child already knows and understands.

Incorporate concrete materials and examples whenever possible, especially with younger children. Try to help your child learn about the subject in more than one way, using as many senses as possible.

Separate your child's school weaknesses from your child. If your child fails a test he or she is not a failure.

Never do your child's homework! (deliberately repeated)

QUESTIONS TO ASK AT PTA MEETING

- Is my child performing at grade level in basic skills? Above/ Below? Math/Reading?
- What are the objectives my child is supposed to attain? How do these objectives lead to the overall goal for the course/grade?

- What achievement, intelligence, or vocational aptitude tests have been given to my child in the past year? What do the scores mean? (Be very specific and be sure you understand completely what the reported scores mean).
- What are my child's strengths and weaknesses in major subject areas?
- What subjects do my child enjoy most?
- Can we together go over some examples of my child's class work?
- Does my child need special help in any academic subject?
- Who are my child's friends and how does he or she interact with other children?
- Has my child regularly completed assigned homework?
- Has my child attended class regularly?

Have you observed any changes in learning progress during the year? Has learning improved or declined during the year?

❑❑❑

43

WORK YOURSELF TO SUCCESS

Feltham says, "The greatest results in life are usually attained by simple means and exercise of ordinary qualities. These may for the most part be summed up in two—common sense and perseverance."

In other words, the surest way to succeed is to determine not to fail.

There are other factors, ways to succeed is to determine not to fail.

Success will remain a stranger to you if you play host to worries. You will never be able to concentrate on the job in hand. Worry will consume a lot of energy. You will give only crumbs of your energy to your main task—of achieving success in life.

A man engulfed in worries is like the engine of a car locked in the garage. The engine is running and consuming fuel. The car does not move an inch. The running engine fouls the atmosphere with poisonous gas. This is the case with the worrying man. He consumes energy. But he does not move an inch towards his goal.

Do away with the habit of 'thinking' too much or brooding. Make up your mind and then act. Action is the greatest antidote to worry, which is nothing but a sort of pessimistic inaction.

Learn to control your thoughts. Never lose sight of the vital fact that worse seldom comes to worst. If you adopt these as your mottos, you will have taken a significant step towards success.

Improve the quality of your work. The secret of success lies in first-rate performance. Slipshod and slovenly bring failure.

You cannot improve your performance if you look upon your work as drudgery. What you do is a part of yourself, an expression of what you stand for. The way you perform your job reveals the inner man in you.

Look upon your job, not as an unpleasant necessity, but as a means of expressing the best in you. William Hazlitt, the famous English writer, has written in one of his essays, "What have I been doing all my life? Have I been idle, or have I nothing to show for all my labour and pain? Is there one thing in which I can challenge competition that can be brought as an instance of exact perfection in which others cannot find a flaw?"

Repeat these questions to yourself, answer them honestly and find out whether you are successful or not in the real sense of the world.

Great men of the world who have achieved pinnacles of success were not freaks of nature. Success did not fall into their lap for heavens, They sweated for it.

Tolstoy's name is often mentioned as a great writer. But few know that he wrote his manuscripts six times before sending them to the publisher. Samuel Johnson was willing to turn over half a library in search of a single word. Nietzsche sometimes wrote his text fifteen times. Spencer remodeled his System of Philosophy five times. Little wonder they enjoyed success which all envy but few achieve. Hard work is the price of success.

Your life is inextricably linked up with that of others.

Rubbing shoulders with others comprises a major part of your life. If you learn how to live harmoniously with others, you are going to add considerably to the chances of your success.

In this respect bear in mind two basic points which cover most others: never speak ill of another if you can do without it. Always be generous in praise.

If you have the habit of backbiting, try to curtail it by reminding yourself, "How shall I feel if someone were to speak of me like this?" If you have to criticize, use fine, cautious words. You have to criticize, not to damage the reputation of the person. Be discreet and employ restraint.

Praise is the lubricant of life. It facilitates human relationships. It is the mark of a successful man that he does not withhold a compliment when it is due. However, be warned. If overdone, it becomes flattery which is the mark of knave.

"We can do anything we want to do if you stick to it long enough," says Helen Keller.

Simple virtues of tenacity willingness, readiness, alertness, courtesy and hard work will carry you further than mere smartness.

A successful business man was asked by a group of students the secret of his success.

"I jump at opportunity."

"And how do you know of opportunity?"

"I keep jumping."

There is no such thing in life as standing still. We are on the way up or the way down. We all possess a spark which can lead us on to achievement, but this spark must be nourished into a flame by resolution to achieve your goal.

Success is a matter of talent and opportunity but, much more, of concentration and perseverance.

When you have set the real goal before you, next step is to make adequate preparations for its achievements. Until and unless you acquire the necessary education, training or experience to give you the know-how you cannot achieve your goal. One who wants to be a doctor has to undergo training in a medical college, and one who wants to become an advocate has to study law.

Since most of us go through life without a goal, without any purpose, without having any specific objective, we do not care to acquire specialised education. The result is that we live, a purposeless and aimless life.

Now you can very well realise that those who succeeded not only had their cherished goal before them but they also developed the necessary qualifications for its achievement. Every person who aspires to be successful first educates himself to be able to pursue his specific goal.

However, education does not mean simply book learning but also the development of personality, leadership, sociability and a sensitivity to discriminate between the true and false values of life and the ability to imbibe those which lead to harmony and happiness.

You may have chosen your goal. You may have even planned out and prepared yourself with a view to achieving your goal. You may have good health too. Still you may not make any progress towards your goal because you may not have enough drive to work for your goal. Actually success is accomplishing something. It is activity in the right direction.

The difference between an active and an inactive person is simply that the former gets what he wants and for the latter it remains as empty as ever.

A half-hearted attempt, a lukewarm effort might take you a little way toward your goal, but it will never get you far enough to reach it.

When the sportsman puts every ounce of his effort and will into the game, nine times out of ten, he is bound to win the race. A person who puts a constant prod on himself and makes an all-out effort is more likely to succeed than the one who makes half-hearted attempts.

One of the reasons why people do not rise above whatever job or work they may be doing is that they have no drive, no will to work. They do not make an all-out effort. They work leisurely, poke around, sit down and gossip, or simply do nothing. And there is no wonder if they do not make an outstanding progress. Without an all-out effort no one can hope to be successful.

Not only an all-out effort is necessary for success, it is also vital that you should be able to maintain the tempo, keep the drive intact till the goal is achieved.

There is the story of the gold prospector who bought a promising piece of rocky land and continuously for five years he mined the land. Everyday he would go down to deepen the tunnel he had made. But there was no sign of gold in sight. One day his patience gave in; his desire for gold became dead. He threw away his mining tools and sold his land to another prospector for a song. The new prospector enlarged the mine only a few inches more and there he found a large seam of gold running through the rock!

Had the first prospector persevered a little more, held on for a few inches more he would have surely found what he was after. "Majority of people is ready to throw their aims and purposes overboard, and give up at the first sign of opposition or misfortune. A few carry on despite all opposition, until they attain their goal," says Napoleon Hill.

Thus for success it is not enough that you should have drive and stamina but persistence too. Persistence is the main force which sustains your drive and makes you go on working for your goal through thick and thin. The quality of persistence "is to the character of man what carbon is to steel.'

In this world, everything perishes and will perish, but, ideas, ideals and dreams do not.

❑❑❑

44

ENJOY YOURSELF WHILE YOU GROW

Humour has been defined variously by various people but everybody agrees that its physical manifestation is a smile or laughter. Kant said that the cause of laughter was "the sudden transformation of a tense expectation into nothing." Henri Bergson says it is "the feeling of relief." With humour, we can establish a congenial atmosphere for ourselves as well as others who come in contact with us. This helps greatly in times of stress and enables us to come out of many a crisis unscarred.

We can do ourselves a lot of good if we remember that except in case of stark tragedy there is always a humorous side to every aspect of life. Humour also serves as a kind of ego booster. A tale about people can be told to show that they are ignorant and thus assure us of our own superiority, if the superiority is just a supposed one, then the comic effect is higher still. It takes a lot of large heartedness for a person to be able to laugh at his own self. When a person realizes that the joke is on him and even then enjoys it, laughs at it, be considered a beneficiary of humour.

The fact is that life is too serious to be taken seriously, unless we can develop the lighter side of our natures, the tragedy of life will overwhelm us. The flippant are to balance grief. Laughter is needed to atone for tears. A sense of humour prevents a man from inflating himself with an absurd dignity. It saves him from being laughed at. It enables him to be a man among men. The man who conceives of himself as an idol has few worshippers.

"Laugh and the world laughs with you; weep, and you alone weep." No one would pay to see the most dignified man in the world, but people pay hundreds of millions to see comedians. In the handling of audience, every effective speaker has found that by the use of humour a crowd of people can be welded into a unit. An audience, too, can be "heated". It must be relaxed and warmed into sympathy with the speaker by his wit and humour. A cold audience sits critical and unconvinced. People are brightened up. They begin to give attrition. They forget their suspicions. They cease being on their guard.

Their natures are changed as much as the nature of iron is when it is made red-hot. Man is said to be the crown of creation for he is endowed with several faculties which distinguish him from the lower species. One such faculty is his ability to laugh. A smiling nature increases our strength. It also adds to our efficiency. A man who 'sings' at his work accomplishes more in the same time and does it better than the stony-head.

A sense of humour acts like a tonic in social life. It increases warmth and lubricates our relationship with other human beings. Thus, it enriches social life. "There is nothing like fun, is there? We need all the counter-weights we can muster to balance sad relations of life. God has made sunny spots in the hearts; why should we exclude the light from them?"

❑❑❑

45

ADJUSTMENT IN NEW SCHOOL

There are certain transitions in life which are quite frightening. The prospect of an uncertain change is one of these changes. When a family moves to a new home, there are certain transitions which will take place, such as a new school for the children. As a child, how should you deal with this new school? What can you do to make the best of it?

Until you understand the layout of the new land, attempt to fit in, and fall back. Despite the fact that you might have some new threads, be bland to keep from being marked. Stay quiet but sweet, and wait for others to approach you. Instead of attempting bold stunts to get noticed, let your natural persona and kindness attract others to you.

How your teachers feel about you will affect your academic pursuits for the rest of your career at this particular school. It is important that your teachers feel that you are a studious, quiet, goal-oriented person. Don't worry about being labeled as a geek, for your natural coolness will prevail. Stay after and ask questions, try to truly understand what your teacher is explaining.

After your first week at school, it is time to start boldly approaching others and leaving your mark on society. Lunch is the prime time to make your move. Approach the same-sex group of kids at their table, which has a few empty spaces, and ask politely if this seat is taken. Once you sit down, have a comment to make about the cafeteria food, particularly the mystery meat. Then feel free to open up the conversation by asking what there is to do in town.

After lunch, dissolve out of the group to keep from being labeled a follower. Now, if possible, it is time to approach the different people one by one. This approach is needed because it keeps them from having the ability to team up as a group against you. Instead they are forced individually to get to know the inner you.

It is important not to form strong liaisons with cliques of people before you know what you are getting into. If you get associated as one type of person, you will be forever type cast. Make friends with everybody, just don't consider one group of people your best friends until you are certain to know who they are.

So the key to fitting in at a new school is treating everybody with the same level of respect and kindness. Don't put a teacher down just to look good to your new friends. At the same time, don't bond too quickly, it is likely to come back and haunt you. Blend in at the beginning until you know how things work in your new environment.

TIPS

Here are few useful tips for the parents. It will ensure that your kids and you have a great time.

- Eat a good breakfast every morning, don't let them skip breakfast.
- Wake them up early enough to get up on time so they are not tardy! Even if that means waking them up 15 or 30 minutes earlier than they used to wake up.
- Be sure your child gets a good night's sleep.
- Have them prepare all of their things the night before, including clothes or uniforms, socks, shoes, bag, homework assignments in bag, etc. down to the finest details, even hair accessories.
- Children should keep their bags, desks and rooms organized so they can find what they need easily and nothing gets lost.
- Praise your children, encourage them, use positive reinforcement, and work closely with them. Let them know that you are available to help, if needed.

- Create a study routine for your child. A good 'rule of thumb' is for them to have their homework right when they get home.
- Go over homework together.
- Check their bags for notes, missed assignments, book orders, etc.
- Promote healthy habits like healthy snacks, low in sugar, fresh fruits and vegetables.
- Children should ask questions. Don't be afraid to ask questions. That is how we learn.
- A stress free child is a happy child. A happy child will do better in school.
- Children should start reviewing notes at least three days before a test. Don't wait until the night before or worse, the day of the test to study for it.
- Children should write down their assignments carefully. Have the number of a few classmates in case you forget to write it down.
- Parents, be a role model to your children. Your children learn from you. Be positive and supportive of the school system and teachers.
- Have your child read to you often and regularly.
- Have them put all of their things in their room right when they get home. This will alleviate the chances of losing or misplacing something. More time is wasted looking for a lost shoe or where they put their bag.
- Children should take notes when the teacher repeats something, tells them to write it down or that is very important or will be on a test, or if she writes it on the board.
- Don't cheat, don't be lazy, do your projects and assignments like reports, ahead of time. Study and learn. You will be proud of yourself.
- During tests, read all of the directions, follow directions, read the questions carefully, and double check your answers if you have time after you have done.

❑❑❑

46

SCHOOL/CAMPUS VIOLENCE

Two to three decades ago the biggest problems in the lives of teachers and students in our school systems were things such as: gum chewing, forgetting a pen/pencil, bunking classes and excessive talking. Today, teachers and students only wish their problems were so trivial. Recently, in a public school in NCR two class VIII students shot dead their classmate on a petty issue. In Western countries, particularly in the USA this kind of school/campus violence is common. The incident of Virginia Tech University is still fresh in our minds. Recently, two Indian scholars were brutally murdered in Louisiana University campus. Indiscriminate firing by teens with sophisticated weapons in crowded business places and Malls are common there.

But in Indian environment such kind of incident is really shocking. Parents, students, school faculty, and even politicians have different opinions as to why our children bring guns/weapons to school to solve conflicts. Majority of people feel that if children had better parental supervision in the home then they would be less likely to lash out at their peers. School educators believe that bad parenting and the family that is uninvolved with the school and/or their own child's education is to blame. Still, other opinions point to environment and a child's exposure to violence through the mass media. Politicians tend to voice same opinion however, they also try to help in finding solutions to the problem.

Learning to understand our children and their needs is the first step in obtaining a solution to violence in school. A child that behaves violently, more often than not, has been a victim of physical violence themselves. Children learn by watching adults and how they behave in society. When an adult acts physically to solve a problem, children see that violent act and take away the message that it is okay to be abusive in order to get what they want. This is a behaviour that most parents do not want to echo throughout the life of their child.

Therefore, instead of teaching our children about hitting/attacking, we should teach them skills that will cause healing, compromise, and resolution.

Once a child feels isolated by their society, friends, and/or family, he or she will begin to show signs of being neglected by lashing out verbally, emotionally, or physically toward others. Many psychologists see this strictly as a behavioral problem caused by a child wanting adult attention. The child does not care whether or not that attention is bad or good as long as the feelings of neglect and isolation are remedied. If a child continually lashes out and is never given the attention they long for, soon they will go into survival mode. Survival mode is when a child has feelings of rejection that grows deep anger within them and ultimately gives them a reprobate mind set. Their consciousness is severed from rational thought process and they begin to have feelings of hatred whom they ultimately harm.

The misguided ness of adult role models in a child's life is also a contributing factor in a violent and aggressive behaviour of a child. A child can become confused when he/she sees an adult handling the wrong and right differently in the same situation. For example a child watching their own parent exhibiting signs of road rage i.e. the parent yelling and threatening the other drivers in a busy traffic area. However, the driver next to them seems unaffected by other drivers. Yet, even another driver impatiently maneouvers their vehicle almost causing a wreck. Whose behaviour will the child later imitate? Most likely, it will be the parent's example that the child will follow in the future. Children are victims and products of their environment, therefore, they must be taught the responsibility of right and wrong not only at home but in society. How can a parent do this? Simple, talk to your kids frequently, and watch their behaviour. If it needs modification, you will know and can solve the problem as soon as it begins.

The lack of supervision at home and school breeds in a child's tendency to misbehave with others. It is impossible to supervise over a child throughout 24 hours. However, it is important that you give your child time, understanding and love. They need these things in order to survive and grow up to be mentally healthy adults. It is a misconception that children that come from impoverished families are most likely to be the violent offenders in school. It is true that many low income families do struggle daily to meet their necessary living needs and that this struggle does produce stress in the household. In this type of surroundings an impoverished child can begin to feel neglected by their parents because they work too long or too hard. However, in upper class homes where the parents bow to every whim of the child can be just as harmful. Many times the child will feel that they should always get what they want and will lash out physically if things don't go their way. Middle class families are no exception to violence either. The very fact that most middle class families have a little source of income. It means that a middle class parent has less time to spend with their children resulting in neglect. That neglect can lead to the middle class child acting out to get attention. Parents need to offer their children strong, positive guidance, discipline and leave time for nurturing.

Violent acts in school/campus most frequently occur from male students. Students have deduced that there are three reasons for most violent acts in school. First, they agree with society's opinion that violent children have poor parental supervision. Secondly, they believe that influence or peer pressure from friends, groups, memberships, and/or gangs is a strong instigator to violent acts indulged in by students. Thirdly, they consider the effects that drugs and alcohol have on their lives and believe it too could be a contributing factor.

School violence is usually targeted toward students between the sixth and twelfth grades. However, a minority in this group is more likely to be physically assaulted than any other of their peers. Teachers are also victims of school violence and tend to feel less safe out of the shadow of the education system. Our children have placed fear into our schools and because of this fear the quality of education has been affected. Inadequate education leaves students frustrated, which can lead to delinquency, anti-social behaviour, and criminal acts. These three side effects will eventually lead to physical violence.

So what can be done to prevent your child from becoming violent in school? Parents should spare time to help their child develop into a productive member of society. Talking with your children is a good start. Answer their questions as honestly as you can. Teach them clearly the difference between right and wrong and give them good problem solving skills. A parent's example can say more to a child than a thousand conversations so let your actions speak louder than your words. Home is the best place to give your child morals and ethics that they will later take with them into their school environment.

Schools have taken on the challenge of solving the problem of violence in school. Solutions that not only make all children safe in their teaching environment but also make them better citizens within the community. Extremely violent students are sent for counseling, refresher programmes, or they perform community service. Most schools have guards at their main entry. Schools add to this security by putting up fences and blocking access to roads. Also, they have begun to lock and chain doors that should not be accessed by students. Teachers and parents visiting as teacher's aides, help to monitor students for discipline problems. School counsellors are on site to talk with students and help them resolve their problems. Ideas such as these can help students feel safer within their own environment.

Remedies to prevent school violence are growing everyday. Our children should be safe in their learning environment and not live in fear that one of their classmates will assault them or even kill them. If the problem of school violence is not solved eventually these violent students will become tomorrow's citizens. Citizens that don't differentiate right from wrong, who do not care whom they harm, and who must get attention. This is not how we view the future of the younger generation. Therefore, we must teach our children at a young age right and wrong, problem solving, and also show them the right way to live by our own examples of the lives we lead before them. It is up to all of us (parents, students, school faculty, and government) to give our children a brighter future and to show them a better way.

TIPS FOR PARENTS

As a parent, one must take pro-active steps to kindle one's child's curiosity, which subsequently will sharpen his/her intellect.

Sometimes children can be lazy, but as a parent there is a lot you can do to improve their interest in academics and the world around them. Encourage your child to collect odds and ends like leaves, rocks, shells, flowers and introduce them to other 'interesting' living species of the planet. This is a way to familiarize the child with its environment and will go a long way in helping him/her understand and learn subjects better. Another way to pep up a study session is to introduce the child to specialties of various regions. For instance, rugs are the specialty of Iran, spices that of India, coffee is the specialty of Brazil, etc. This way the child's retention capacity is widened as he can identify places and their importance more easily. Also encourage your child to read a lot, be it fiction, travelogues or non-fiction. Nothing broadens a child's already imaginative mind like books.

For a parent, it is most important to remember that academics and text books are not necessarily the only or the best tools to give a child good education. Develop an interest in the world around you and you will automatically pass this on to your child. The real world can teach lessons to a child, he may never learn in school.

HELP CHILD, BUILD SELF-ESTEEM

It is important that the child takes pride in what s/he is doing and not gets disheartened by small failures. Help the child look at him/herself from an objective perspective. Encourage the child to write a book about him/herself, which enumerates qualities and drawbacks. What is important here is that the child should be taught to be honest about himself instead of trying to put a veil over drawbacks or hype up virtues. Allow the child to know more about him/herself by speaking with seniors and elders in the family. This way even s/he will be aware of the family tree as also learn values and qualities from others that should be emulated.

❑❑❑

47

POCKET-MONEY

"How should I give my children pocket-money?" is one of the most common questions asked at parenting seminars.

"Should kids receive pocket-money when they complete jobs and should they lose pocket-money if they are poorly behaved?" are also common queries.

Giving pocket-money is an excellent way to develop independence in children and young people.

Here are five ideas to help you use pocket-money to develop independence and also a sense of generosity in your children:

1.Give pocket-money regularly: Like adults children should have a pay day each week or fortnight or month when they receive their share.

2.Use the three jars concept: Provide three jars for children when you give them pocket-money–one for spending, one for saving/investing and one for charity. Ask children to distribute their pocket-money among the jars. Giving children coins rather than notes makes this activity easier. This is a fascinating activity which gives you the chance to teach kids a great deal about money and its use. For instance, you can get across the idea of saving before spending *i.e.* setting aside an amount of money for saving/investing rather than saving what they have left over at the end of the week. You can also introduce them to the notion of setting aside some of your income for charitable purposes. You may want to have a rule or procedure that states once money is allocated to a jar it is not retrieved later!

3. Link pocket-money to age and stage of development and their needs (not wants): Provide guidelines about spending including letting them know just what they are expected to buy. A child in pre-school and lower primary school may get enough to purchase some sweets and one or two other items, whereas a child in upper primary school may get enough to cover lunch orders, bus money and some treats. An allowance that covers clothing can be useful for adolescents who can be very costly to outfit in the latest fashions.

4. You can pay me back later: If you get sick of your children asking you for treats or even the latest fad or gadget suggest that they can make a purchase or at least make a contribution from their personal wealth. If you are pestered at the supermarket to buy an ice cream or some such treat you can say, "Certainly you can have an ice cream out of your own money. If you haven't any money with you I'll buy it and you can pay me back when we get home."

5. Teach kids about goal-setting: By encouraging children to save for a big ticket item (or even make a contribution) such as a bike or skateboard children learn a great deal about planning and looking ahead, the value of budgeting and experience personal satisfaction of reaching a goal.

When used wisely, pocket-money is an excellent way to develop independence in children and young people. And by the way, it may be smart to cut or reduce pocket-money when they turn fifteen and encourage them to get a part-time job so they begin to pay their own way.

Whether you give your children pocket money is a decision for your family.

Advantages of pocket money can be that children:

- develop a sense of how much has to be done to earn money
- learn that 'money doesn't grow on trees'
- learn what money can buy - how much they need to buy what they want
- can have their own money to spend - helping them to develop self control and understanding the value of money

- learn about saving
- will know there is a set amount of money rather than asking for money all the time.

Disadvantages can be that:

- children may think they will get paid for everything they do to help
- you have to find the money to pay them regularly
- it is hard to know what the pocket money is supposed to pay for—there always seems to be something more.

If you decide to give pocket money you need to work out:

- how much is reasonable
- whether the money will be paid for doing chores
- how much must be done to earn it—and how much is simply because 'you are a member of the family'
- how much each job is worth
- whether all children get the same amount or the older child gets more
- how much control parents will have over the use of pocket money—do they have to save some? What can they buy with it?
- when will you pay—the children won't learn about the responsibility of money if you don't honour the agreement.

An idea might be to give your child a set amount each week, putting half in a savings account.

- At the end of a time agreed on by you both—perhaps three months—the child can spend the saved money exactly as they wish.
- If they choose to 'waste' it on chocolates or ice-cream they can do so.
- However most children want something special and usually prefer to save for that particular thing and not waste it on a brief pleasure.
- This helps to teach them the value of saving.

HOW MUCH POCKET MONEY

- The value of money is its buying power. You need to work out how much things cost now, particularly the things your children will want to buy.
- Be realistic and increase the amount as your child becomes ready for the responsibility. Keep track of their expenses by monitoring what they buy for a week or two. Give them enough for the basics and a little bit more but not enough that they could buy anything they wanted.
- When children are little the basics might mean how much you spend on treats for them each week. Having to spend their own money for treats lets them learn that treats are special and limited.
- By about the age of 10 or 11 you might give them enough to pay for their lunch at school and treats. By 13 they might be required to pay for treats, lunch and transport. You can then slowly add responsibility for clothes, entertainment and gifts for other people.

When children begin earning their own money you need to think about pocket money again. Should they get the pocket money as well?

❑❑❑

48

NO CELL PHONNE FOR HIGH SCHOOL STUDENTS

Children now have it so easy in some ways, and so much harder in others. Although access to information is now available at your child's fingertips and communication has become so much more efficient thanks to the cellular phones, competition has heated up and a child has to be much more focused and driven to succeed than he needed to be a couple of generations ago.

Another flip side of easy access to communication, is easy access to material you would rather your child didn't have access to—and, the misuse of such material.

PORN

MMS porn clips are all the rage, and recently objectionable pictures are doing the rounds. Many parents feel that they should not give their teenage child a cell-phone that has a camera. The potential for misuse is high, and even if your child is not someone who would take obscene images with his cell camera and forward it to all his friends, he may very easily receive such an MMS from his friends.

Just by denying your child a cell phone with a camera doesn't mean that your child will not be able to view these images. Even if your child cannot receive them on his phone, he will be able to view them on his friend's phones. However, chances are that your child may see these images on a friend's phone just from the point of view of fascination, and will soon put them out of his mind. But in his own phone he may be tempted to store them, view them over and over again, and when the opportunity presents itself for him to make his own little porn clip, he may excitedly do so. Both total prohibition and easy access are undesirable. Try and find a balance by giving your child a bare cell from which he can only make and receive calls. Also, if you are worried that your child will spend a lot of money making calls, you can very easily set a limit by providing your child with a cash card, and letting him know that if the card runs out, you will not be giving him money for a new card until the end of the month.

RESPONSIBILITY

Not only will this discourage needless usage of the phone, but your child will be tempted to make less outgoing calls and use the phone more for incoming calls. If your child does run out of his cash card in the middle of the month, let him know that he can use his own pocket money to recharge the amount. Alternatively, you can get your child a phone, and tell him that he will need to use his pocket money to pay his phone bills. This will encourage your child to save his money, to budget himself and to account for it wisely and responsibly, from a young age.

SAFETY

Some parents think that it is totally unnecessary for their children to have cell phones, while other parents would like their children to carry phones because it is easy for parents to trace them. Also, parents worry less now, because if their child is getting late, he can always call home and let his parents know that whether he is stuck in a traffic jam or he needs to stay back for basketball practice. However, earlier parents had no option but to sit at home and worry, or call other parents, trying desperately to find out why their child is late.

Cell phones should absolutely be banned from school, no qestions asked. We lived without them since long and we can live for years without them if we chose to do so. They are nothing but a disruption to class instruction. The student (if he or she is waiting for a call) thinks about nothing but receiving that call, therefore blocking out anything that is being said, and it's simply not a necessity for being successful in school.

❑❑❑

49

INTERACTION WITH YOUR CHILD'S TEACHER

No parent will forget the day when their children went to school for the first time. Every parent has a dream about their child's bright future, while sending them to school. However most of the parents ignore the fact that regular interaction with your child's teachers is also important for their academic excellence. It is the parent-teacher relationship that is the most important contributing factor to a child's success at school. Education is not just spoon feeding your children with all the possible general knowledge and skills but, it is knowing your children and helping them to develop their personality to become successful human beings. The essence of education is comprised in sharing responsibility between children, parents and teachers, to promote your child's general well-being and to provide a basis for success.

Researches say that parental involvement in education may be far reaching. A good relationship between the parent, teacher and student allows all three parties to have a shared understanding of learning goals, the curriculum and ways they can work together to achieve the best for the student. It is most important for each parent to know their children's teachers personally and discuss about your child's education regularly. The parent-teacher communication should not be an occasion to reveal parents' dreams and beliefs about a child or for teachers, to open the bundle of complaints about a student. Rather mutual discussion about the drawbacks and ways to improve skills or learning of the child should take place in parent-teacher interaction.

When you discuss about your child to their teachers, always be patient and open enough to listen to the teacher. Viewpoints can differ as parents always see their children through an affectionate eye while a teacher may have an analysing view. Accept, instead of arguing with the teachers if he/she makes a negative comment about your child, and discuss the ways to lead your child to success.

Teacher should know the family atmosphere in which each student is brought up. It will help them to adapt a more psychologically customised approach to each student. The difference a caring and attentive parent can make to a child's life and academic career is magnificent.

It is the duty of a teacher, to let the parents know how their child is doing at school. This actually helps parents to be more responsive to those areas where their child needs work. Making it personal will help parent-teacher interaction more effective than mere formal communication.

It is clear that parents and teachers have the same end goal in mind when it comes to their students. Communicating and sharing about a child will help parents to become better parents and teachers to become successful teachers. Remember always; parent-teacher communication should be focused on the best interests of the child.

When talking with your children's teachers you must give insights into their child's character, strengths, interests, needs and areas of concern. This information may be helpful for a teacher to understand students better and help them to improve their life. Before making an interaction with teachers it is always preferable to discuss with your child the views, they have about their teachers, favourite teacher etc. Try to know how your child feels about his /her school.

Effective parent-teacher communication includes asking questions mutually. Parent can ask about the curriculum, What will be covered in the class this year, how they help and what can be done at home to help children's education etc. The same time teacher can ask about their students learning habits, personal interests, areas of struggle etc. Be regular in your relationship with your children's teacher since it will help you to have a regular analysis of your child's academic growth. The ultimate goal of parent-teacher communication is to know your child from all perspective and help them to improve in all realms of life. Know your child as a human being who has needs, hopes, interests and dreams. Help them to attain their goals and ambitions. Successful parent-teacher interaction must help both parents and teachers to know who the child is, to lend a helping hand in their success.

❑❑❑

50

HANDLING TEENS

Privacy is important to children just as it is to their parents. All children need some space to call their own, where no parents or siblings are pawing around. The wise parent understands this and respects the child's privacy.

Some parents feel absolutely entitled to snoop around in their kids' rooms, open their mail, listen in to their phone conversations, and perform other disrespectful acts.

These acts are usually justified by one of two excuses. "It's my house and I pay the bills around here." or "I have to know what my kid is doing, it's my job to snoop."

But answer honestly. How would you feel if your boss checked your drawer? Your boss pays the rent of the office. Does that give him or her right to snoop?

As far as knowing what your kids are doing, the best way to do that is to have open communication between loving and trusting people. Nobody loves or trusts a snoop.

When the teen years are approaching have a family meeting about respecting each other's privacy.

Spend some time together talking about the difference between private and shared space. Talk about limits like not opening mail or eavesdropping on phone conversations. Ask your children if they want you to put the laundry away in their room or they prefer to do it themselves. Remember kids old enough to want privacy are old enough to do their own laundry!

Respect and trust will keep a teen in line a lot better than snooping and suspicion.

Telephone usage: The problem of teen telephone hogging is very common. The reason the telephone is so important to teens is that friends are so important. The telephone is not only the way teens keep in touch but it is also the way teens 'practice' communication in a safe way. If they blush or overreact or aren't wearing their most fashionable jeans, no one sees. Teens also find it easier to try out new ideas and feelings on the telephone than in person and teens have lots of new ideas and feelings.

Exasperated as parents get when their boss or friends complain that the line is always busy, they should really get worried if the phone never rings for their teenager. A silent telephone indicates a lonely and disconnected child. When the phone rings a lot the teen gets a connecting message from their friends that say you are liked and wanted.

But the home telephone is a utility/resource for the entire family so that there must be rules for sharing. Of course, there are some families that can afford a cell phone for each child. However learning how to share a scarce resource is good for the child and the family also.

Teen's responsibility: When your teenager demands more freedom here is a check list to help both you and your teen to determine whether there is enough responsibility to warrant that freedom.

A responsible teen:

- respects himself/herself
- respects others
- has developed a love of learning
- has learned self-control
- is empathic
- is developing pro-social values
- is kind
- stays in school
- dreams, plans, and prepares for a future
- makes wise choices
- follows the rules and obeys the law
- does not harm self or others
- is building a value system to become a productive, involved citizen
- has a sense of community

❑❑❑